Minnesota Mediterranean and Ea.
Monographs

XVII

INTERNATIONAL AGGRESSION AND VIOLATIONS OF HUMAN RIGHTS

The Case of Turkey in Cyprus

MINNESOTA MEDITERRANEAN AND EAST EUROPEAN MONOGRAPHS

Theofanis G. Stavrou, general editor

1. *Kosovo: Legacy of a Medieval Battle*
   edited by Wayne S. Vucinich and Thomas A. Emmert

2. *Inside the Cyprus Miracle: The Labours of an Embattled Mini-Economy*
   by Demetrios Christodoulou

3. *Modern Greek Word Formation*
   by Olga Eleftheriades

4. *Prelude to the Great Reforms: Avraam Sergeevich Norov and Imperial Russia*
   by Peter R. Weisensel

5. *Blocking the Sun: The Cyprus Conflict*
   by John L. Scherer

6. *Britain and the International Status of Cyprus, 1955-59*
   by Evanthis Hatzivassiliou

7. *A Missionary for History: Essays in Honor of Simon Dubnov*
   edited by Kristi Groberg and Avraham Greenbaum

8. *Cyprus 1957-1963: From Colonial Conflict to Constitutional Crisis:
   The Key Role of the Municipal Issue*
   by Diana Weston Markides

9. *The Gates of Hell: The Great Sobor of the Russian Orthodox Church, 1917-1918*
   by James W. Cunningham, edited by Keith and Grace Dyrud

10. *Russian-Ottoman Relations in the Levant: The Dashkov Archive*
    by Theophilus C. Prousis

11. *The Cyprus Question, 1878-1960: The Constitutional Aspect*
    by Evanthis Hatzivassiliou

12. *Lessons Unlearned: Thucydides and Venizelos on Propaganda
    and the Struggle for Power*
    by Evie Holmberg

13. *Church and State in Late Imperial Russia: Critics of the Synodal
    System of Church Government (1861-1914)*
    by John Basil

14. *War and Cultural Heritage: Cyprus after the 1974 Turkish Invasion*
    by Michael Jansen

15. *Cyprus: A Contemporary Problem in Historical Perspective*
    by Van Coufoudakis

16. *Fettered Independence: Cyprus, 1878–1964*
    by Stella Soulioti

17. *International Aggression and Violations of Human Rights:
    The Case of Turkey in Cyprus*
    by Van Coufoudakis

Minnesota Mediterranean and East European
Monographs

INTERNATIONAL AGGRESSION AND VIOLATIONS OF HUMAN RIGHTS

The Case of Turkey in Cyprus

Van Coufoudakis

MODERN GREEK STUDIES

UNIVERSITY OF MINNESOTA

MINNEAPOLIS, MINNESOTA

Number 17

2008

Minnesota Mediterranean and East European Monographs (MMEEM)

Theofanis G. Stavrou, general editor
Soterios G. Stavrou, associate editor
Elizabeth A. Harry, assistant editor

The objective of the MMEEM is the dissemination of scholarly information about the Mediterranean and East European region. The field is broadly defined to include the social sciences and the humanities. Even though the emphasis of the series is on the Greek and Slavic worlds, there are no thematic, geographical, or chronological limitations. Through the series we hope to encourage research in a variety of contemporary problems in their historical context. In this regard, special efforts will be made to accommodate proceedings from scholarly conferences as well as monographic studies with a diachronic approach.

Monographs in the MMEEM series are published by the Modern Greek Studies Program at the University of Minnesota as supplements to the *Modern Greek Studies Yearbook*. *International Aggression and Violations of Human Rights: The Case of Turkey in Cyprus* by Van Coufoudakis is number 17 in the series. Its publication has been made possible by subvention from the Modern Greek Studies Program at the University of Minnesota.

The price for this volume is $30.00, paperback. Make checks payable to:

Modern Greek Studies
325 Social Science Building
UNIVERSITY OF MINNESOTA
267—19th Avenue South
Minneapolis, MN 55455
Telephone: (612) 624-4526

Library of Congress Control Number: 2008940296
ISSN: 1057-3941
ISBN–13: 978-0-9791218-2-1
ISBN–10: 0-9791218-2-5

Cover: Watercolor and ink (2008) by Julie Delton

The UNIVERSITY OF MINNESOTA is an equal-opportunity employer.
Printed in the United States of America on acid-free paper

To
The People of Cyprus
My wife Marion
And my daughter Helen

CONTENTS

Preface   ix

Chapter One
Cyprus: A Brief Historical Introduction   1

Chapter Two
Human Rights in the Post-World War II International System   7

Chapter Three
Cyprus and the European Human Rights Institutions   15

Chapter Four
Invasion, Continuing Occupation, and Violations
of Personal Rights   31

Chapter Five
Invasion, Occupation, and Ethnic Cleansing:
The Human Dimension   49

Chapter Six
The Continuing Consequences of Ethnic Cleansing: Property
Usurpation, Settlers, and the Destruction of Cultural Heritage   69

Chapter Seven
Cyprus and the European Human Rights Regime:
Concluding Comments   91

Appendix One
European Union Resolutions on Cyprus   95

Appendix Two
United Nations Resolutions on Cyprus   105

Notes   115

Glossary   123

Bibliography   125

Index   131

PREFACE

IN NOVEMBER 2006 my book *Cyprus: A Contemporary Problem in Historical Perspective* was published by the Minnesota Mediterranean and East European Monographs, a series under the auspices of the Modern Greek Studies Program at the University of Minnesota. Friends and colleagues encouraged me to write a companion volume devoted exclusively to human rights issues raised by the 1974 Turkish invasion and continuing occupation of nearly 37 percent of the Republic of Cyprus. These issues have taken added significance because of their continuing nature, because the Republic of Cyprus is a member of the EU, and because the Republic of Turkey commenced EU accession talks in the fall of 2005.

Article VI of the EU founding treaty pays particular attention to human rights issues in the context of the European Convention of Human Rights and the decisions of the European Court of Human Rights. It also defines the obligations of current and prospective members and sets standards of conduct expected of all. This is one of the reasons why this book is timely and relevant.

The human rights issues raised in this volume follow broad definitions of human rights found in contemporary human rights literature. In addition to traditional civil and political rights, the book addresses economic and social rights and the protection of cultural heritage. Specialists as well as readers interested in human rights and committed to the ideal that the protection and promotion of human rights lies at the heart of democracy and the rule of law will find this book of interest.

Most readers are unaware of the significant human rights issues involved in the Cyprus problem, let alone the important decisions and actions taken by European institutions in an attempt to safeguard human rights in Cyprus. The decisions and actions of the European Commission of Human Rights and of the European Court of Human Rights in cases involving Cyprus point to the importance attached to human rights in the European legal and political order. Through my frequent visits to both the free and occupied areas of Cyprus, I have witnessed the consequences of ethnic cleansing and of the confiscation, usurpation, and exploitation of Greek Cypriot property in occupied Cyprus. I have spent hours talking with families of the missing about their anguish and discussed with displaced persons and refugees their longing to return to their ancestral homes in peace and safety. I have observed the demographic impact of Turkish settlers and the tragic living conditions of the enclaved in the Karpass Peninsula. I have also witnessed the destruction of the Greek Cypriot cultural heritage. While teaching in the Indiana University system, I was able to follow the precedent-setting case of the Kanakaria mosaics at the Federal Court in Indianapolis (1998). Turkish Cypriot antiquity smugglers looted these historic religious mosaics dating to the sixth century A.D. from a church in occupied Cyprus. This was done with the complicity of the occupation authorities. Removal of mosaics and frescoes from walls requires technical expertise and local support. The mosaics were illegally sold to an Indianapolis art dealer. They have now been recovered and are back in a religious museum in the land of their origin.

Finally, this book reflects my conviction that no viable solution to the Cyprus problem is possible unless fundamental human rights issues are addressed in the context of European law. The accession of Cyprus to the EU and Turkey's candidacy offer a unique opportunity to resolve this problem of invasion, occupation, and continuing violation of internationally recognized human rights. A solution conforming to EU law and principles will protect the rights of all Cypriots and will strengthen the European institutional and legal framework for the protection of human rights.

I extend my appreciation to Professor Theofanis Stavrou, director of the Modern Greek Studies Program at the University of Minnesota, whose untiring commitment to the field of Modern Greek Studies has made this publication series possible. I also thank Soterios Stavrou for his editorial assistance. His professionalism and constructive suggestions helped to improve this volume. However, the views expressed and any omissions are exclusively those of the author.

Van Coufoudakis
Sarasota, Florida
October 2008

CHAPTER ONE

Cyprus: A Brief Historical Introduction

THE REPUBLIC OF CYPRUS gained its independence from Britain on 16 August 1960, following a four-year anti-colonial rebellion by the Greek Cypriots. Independence was based on a complex set of agreements negotiated by Great Britain,[1] Greece, and Turkey in 1959. Known as the Zurich and London Agreements (1959), these tri-partite agreements were negotiated without the participation of the Greek and the Turkish Cypriot leadership. They have now become a classic case of unequal treaties imposed on the Greek Cypriot majority under the threat of partition of their island. In addition to the complex constitutional provisions that granted extraordinary veto powers to the minority Turkish Cypriot community, Great Britain, Greece, and Turkey became guarantors of the new republic with vaguely defined rights of intervention in the affairs of the new state. Great Britain also retained ninety-nine square miles, i.e. 2.7 percent, of the island, as sovereign base areas. Today, these British bases, in addition to a major airfield, military hospitals, and other logistical facilities, house some of the most sophisticated electronic monitoring facilities in the world. Unofficially shared with the National Security Agency of the United States, these bases remain outside the NATO or the EU Defense network.[2]

Difficulties in the implementation of these agreements led to Greek Cypriot attempts to legally amend the Constitution. Turkey, followed by the Turkish Cypriot leaders, rejected the Greek Cypriot proposals. Intercommunal clashes followed in December 1963, while the Turkish Cypriots withdrew from the institutions of the Republic of Cyprus. A United Nations peacekeeping force (UNFICYP) was dispatched to the Republic of Cyprus in March 1964, with the consent of the government, because of the intercommunal clashes and the threat of a Turkish military intervention.[3] The UN secretary-general was also asked to offer his "good offices" in the search for a solution of the Cyprus problem.

It is important to note that despite the constitutional crisis created by the Turkish Cypriot withdrawal from the government of the Republic of Cyprus, the position of the international community has been consistent and clear. All governments, except that of Turkey, and all international and regional organizations recognize only the Republic of Cyprus, its sovereignty, unity, and territorial integrity. This consistent international position has been reaffirmed by numerous resolutions and actions since then,[4] at critical junctures in the life of the Republic of Cyprus. The latest affirmation of the legitimacy and continuity of the Republic of Cyprus was its signature of the Treaty of Accession to the European Union on 16 April 2003 and the actual accession of the Republic of Cyprus to the EU on 1 May 2004. The Republic of Cyprus created in 1960 is now part of the EU, although the *acquis communautaire* is not applied in areas of the republic under Turkish occupation.

On 20 July 1974, following a coup against the government of the Republic of Cyprus organized by the junta ruling Greece at the time, Turkey invaded and occupied 37 percent of the territory of the republic in a two-phase invasion. The UN Security Council adopted various resolutions calling for the respect of the territorial integrity, independence, and sovereignty of Cyprus, for a ceasefire, and for an end to hostilities. Turkey disregarded all of these unanimous resolutions. Even though Turkey's stated objective for its invasion of Cyprus was the restoration of the *status quo ante*, Turkey has systematically attempted to partition Cyprus, a plan in the works since the early 1950s.

The Turkish occupation continues at this time and Cyprus remains the last divided and occupied country of Europe. When Cyprus joined the EU, the goal of the reunification of the republic had not been achieved. In 1999, at the Helsinki summit, the leaders of the European Union unanimously agreed that Cyprus would become a member of the EU with or without a solution to the political problem. Had they acted differently, they would have given Turkey, a non-EU member, veto over EU enlargement policy and would have held Cyprus hostage to Turkish policy. It should be remembered that years of mediation initiatives under the "good offices" of the UN secretary-general had failed to resolve the Cyprus problem. This deadlock was due to the fact that Turkey and its allies aimed at the imposition of a divisive political solution that failed to address the consequences of the 1974 Turkish invasion of Cyprus and violated the European human rights regime.[5] A basic thesis of the present volume is that the Cyprus problem was and remains one of invasion, continuing occupation, and violation of internationally recognized human rights, a violation of the international legal order of post-Cold War Europe. This theme will be elaborated in the discussion of European political and legal institutions included in chapter two. In addition, Turkey's actions constitute a threat to regional stability, at a time when Turkey, with the support of Greece and Cyprus, has opened accession negotiations with the European Union.

There is no doubt that there is a domestic dimension to the Cyprus problem. Seeking a functional constitutional formula that will overcome the dysfunctional provisions of the 1960 Cypriot constitution has been the primary objective of the intercommunal talks held under the "good offices" of the UN secretary-general since 1964.

In order to be accepted by the majority Greek Cypriot community, any resolution plan must conform to the standards of European law and to the human rights and other obligations of Cyprus under the European Convention and the Charter of Fundamental Freedoms of the European Union. It must also allow the Republic of Cyprus to meet its obligations under international and EU law.

Since 1974, Turkey and its allies have attempted to reduce the Cyprus problem to a simple intercommunal conflict requiring constitutional resolution.

This approach, inevitably, views the protection of human rights as the outcome of a political settlement likely to be based on ethnic separation, in order to avoid recurrence of intercommunal strife. However, this simplistic approach aims at protecting Turkey from the consequences of its actions in Cyprus since 1974. As stated earlier, the Cyprus problem was and remains one of invasion, continuing occupation, and violation of internationally recognized human rights. Failure to address that reality has driven the Cyprus problem to its current stalemate and has provided excuses for Turkey's documented and continuing violations of international and European law.

This study will discuss the violations of human rights caused by the 1974 Turkish invasion and continuing occupation of 37 percent of the Republic of Cyprus. These violations have been documented by various international and regional organizations, nongovernmental organizations, international court decisions, eyewitness accounts, and so on. These violations are even more striking considering the small size of the island of Cyprus (3,572 square miles) and its population. There is hardly anyone who has not been affected by Turkey's 1974 invasion and by the consequences of that invasion. In summary form, the consequences of the Turkish invasion include, but are not limited to:

- the forcible expulsion of some 170,000 Greek Cypriots, about 28 percent of the total population of the republic in 1974, from their ancestral homes. At that time, Greek Cypriots constituted 70 percent of the population in the area currently under Turkish military occupation. Greek Cypriots are still not allowed to return to their homes and properties, despite decisions by the European Court of Human Rights. In turn, Turkish Cypriots living in the free areas were forced to move to the occupied areas by 1975 under threat by their leadership and the Turkish Army. Therefore, ethnic cleansing was one of the major consequences of the Turkish invasion. This action affected nearly half of the total population of Cyprus. To understand the magnitude of this event, it would have been as if 120 million Americans were forced to relocate in a matter of few months in 1974.
- the nearly 1,600 persons, including civilians, that remain missing. When last seen, most of these persons were in Turkish custody. It is only after thirty years that Turkey is cooperating in ascertaining the fate of these persons. It should be noted that the Committee on Missing Persons can only identify remains through DNA methods, without investigating the cause of death or identifying the party or parties responsible for their death. Nor is the committee authorized to carry out investigations in Turkey, where many of the missing were transported after the Turkish invasion. The number of the Cypriot missing, in proportion to the population of Cyprus in 1974, is overwhelming.
- the nearly five hundred Greek and Maronite Cypriots that remain enclaved in their villages in the Karpass Peninsula of Northeast Cyprus. These persons are living under conditions of oppression, fear, intimidation, and deprivation, conditions that have been documented by independent sources.

- the military and political control of the occupied areas by some 40,000 heavily armed Turkish troops. They are supported from logistical bases in southern Turkey, some forty miles north of Cyprus. These troops are armed with American and NATO weapons.

- the conclusions of the first two Cypriot interstate applications against Turkey, by the European Commission of Human Rights. The commission determined that the Turkish troops committed looting, rape, forced detentions, murder, torture, deportations of civilians, and property confiscation in occupied Cyprus.

- the major economic dislocation. Nearly 70 percent of the economic output of Cyprus (minerals, agriculture, tourism) came from areas under Turkish military occupation. Cypriot Gross Domestic Product dropped by 33 percent, while unemployment rose to 29.6 percent in contrast to 1.2 percent prior to the Turkish invasion.

- the control by the Turkish Army of major cities like Famagusta and its environs, Kyrenia, and Morphou, along with 197 villages.

- the forced migration of approximately 3.4 percent of the Greek Cypriot population, primarily from the ranks of the displaced. They were forced to migrate to Europe and Australia in search of work and safety.

- consequences difficult to quantify: These included poverty, shortage of adequate housing for the displaced, dislocation of social organization, shortage of adequate medical facilities and schools, community disintegration, and family break-up. The social impact was particularly severe since Cyprus's society is so closely knit.

- the impact of approximately 160,000 settlers from Turkey's Eastern Anatolian region who have been relocated into occupied Cyprus. These persons are not economic refugees. They were dispatched to occupied Cyprus under a deliberate Turkish government policy intended to alter the demography of the Turkish Cypriot community and of Cyprus as a whole. This deliberate colonization policy violates the provisions of the 1949 Geneva Convention. One of the consequences of this colonization policy has been the mass Turkish Cypriot exodus to countries like Germany and Great Britain. At this time, the settlers outnumber the native Turkish Cypriots by a ratio of 2:1.

- the systematic destruction of the Greek Cypriot cultural heritage. Churches have been looted and destroyed and ancient and religious artifacts have been looted and sold in the international black market for art objects, while archaeological sites have been destroyed. Historical names of cities and villages in occupied Cyprus have also been erased and replaced by Turkish names.

- the systematic and documented usurpation of Greek Cypriot property in occupied Cyprus. This has resulted in precedent-setting cases brought against Turkey by Greek Cypriots in the European Court of Human Rights.

- the determination by European human rights institutions that Turkey's actions in occupied Cyprus were directed against Greek Cypriots because of their ethnicity, language, and religion. This violated the non-discrimination provision (article 14) of the European Convention.

This list is not exhaustive. It shows, however, the seriousness of the consequences of the Turkish invasion of Cyprus and of the violations of major international treaties that Turkey signed and ratified. These issues will be discussed and documented in this volume. As my earlier work on Cyprus has shown, there can be no viable solution to the Cyprus problem unless fundamental human rights issues are addressed in their proper European legal and political context. The restoration and protection of human rights cannot wait for a political settlement of the Cyprus problem; rather, it must be the foundation of any viable political settlement. The Republic of Cyprus is now a member of the European Union, while Turkey is a candidate state for EU accession. This is why a solution of the Cyprus problem must conform to European human rights standards and laws, bring to an end the continuing violations of Greek Cypriot human rights, and restore the rights of all those affected by the 1974 Turkish invasion and continuing occupation.

Cyprus from Antiquity to 1878

The recorded history of the island of Cyprus dates back to 9,000 B.C. Mycenaean and Achaean Greeks brought Greek culture and civilization to Cyprus around 1,200 B.C. Since then, and despite many conquests, Cyprus retained its Hellenic character and culture. The island's vibrant Hellenic kingdoms contributed to the culture and history of the ancient Hellenic world.

Because of its important strategic location, Cyprus has been affected by the actions of powers that have dominated the eastern Mediterranean. Cyprus became a province of the Roman Empire (30 B.C.–330 A.D.) and a province of the Byzantine Empire (330–1191), and came under the control of the Crusaders, the French Lusignans, and the Venetians (1191–1571). From 1571 to 1878 Cyprus was part of the Ottoman Empire. This was a major turning point in the long history of Cyprus. Cypriot culture, society, and political development were permanently altered by Ottoman rule. The Ottomans introduced a Turkish minority, the Turkish language, and the Islamic faith to an otherwise homogeneous Hellenic and Christian territory. In 1878, Cyprus came under British rule and remained a British colony until 1960. It should be noted that peaceful bicommunal coexistence was the norm during most of the period of Ottoman and British rule, a fact attested by the demographic distribution of the two communities across Cyprus until the 1974 Turkish invasion.

Objectives of this Volume

The Cyprus Question has generated an extensive bibliography on various aspects of the problem. This brief study brings together substantive information on the human rights consequences of the Turkish invasion and continuing occupation of Cyprus, Turkey's failure to comply with decisions of international organizations and courts, and the impact of Turkey's defiance of the international legal order. Turkey's defiance raises serious questions about the commitment of influential actors to the protection and promotion of human rights. Clearly, human rights have been subordinated to economic, political, and security considerations, despite the importance ascribed to human rights since the end of the Cold War. The present volume should appeal to specialists as well as those committed to the protection and promotion of human rights.

The events of 1974 brought about the documented, massive, and continuing violations of human rights by Turkey in Cyprus. In view of other more current international crises, the 1974 events on Cyprus may be considered as obsolete by some observers. However, these issues retain their currency and their relevancy in view of the evolution of the institutional mechanisms and procedures created for the protection and promotion of human rights by the Council of Europe, the European Union, and the OSCE. Moreover, the continuing violations of human rights by Turkey in Cyprus, and Turkey's defiance of political and juridical decisions by European institutions on Cyprus and aspirations for membership in the European Union make this book a necessary reading in the first decade of the twenty-first-century.

CHAPTER TWO

Human Rights in the Post-World War II International System

WHILE the philosophical foundations of human rights can be traced to antiquity, declaratory human rights public policy statements came much later in human history. The 1689 English Bill of Rights, the 1878 French Declaration of the Rights of Man and the Citizen, and the 1776 American Declaration of Independence are examples of the incorporation of human rights principles in major political documents and declarations. Most writers agree that the modern conception of rights originated in Western European and American thought, an issue that raised claims of "cultural imperialism"[1] in the early days of post-World War II decolonization and during the Cold War. This debate originated in conflicting modern philosophical approaches to human rights issues. Proponents of economic and social rights challenged the traditional liberal Wilsonian approach, especially in the aftermath of the Communist Revolution in Russia. This became the precursor of the post-World War II human rights debate.

The 1948 United Nations Universal Declaration of Human Rights (UDHR), the "Magna Carta" of human rights,[2] attempted to synthesize the two philosophical approaches. Ratified by fifty of the then fifty-eight members of the United Nations, the UDHR was only a declaration by contracting states and not a binding treaty. Even so, Eleanor Roosevelt had to work hard to gain the endorsement of the Truman administration for the inclusion of socioeconomic rights in this declaration. Since then, the UDHR principles have become part of customary law. They have also become the foundation of much of the human rights legislation subsequently adopted in treaty form by the United Nations and by regional institutions such as the Council of Europe.

The United Nations Charter was a document based on political compromise. Article 55 linked the protection of human rights to peace.[3] The charter also included generic references to human rights in its preamble and in Article 1. However, during the Cold War, despite the adoption by the UN of many human rights conventions,[4] its work in the field of human rights was stymied by political considerations that became part of the wider East-West ideological struggle. The politicization of human rights during the Cold War undercut the legitimacy of efforts to protect and promote human rights globally.

In sharp contrast, Western Europe, with its cultural and political cohesiveness, moved quickly and consciously to build a regional human rights regime with appropriate enforcement mechanisms that will be discussed below. The end of the Cold War and the emerging European unification brought about the convergence of human rights, democracy, and the rule of law.[5]

The United Nations and the European institutions that were created in the aftermath of World War II did not have to reinvent the wheel in terms of collective action in the field of human rights. There were ample precedents from the nineteenth century. Some were intended to stop massacres of Christian minorities in the Ottoman Empire;[6] others involved actions outlawing the slave trade or implementing humane rules in warfare. However, these sporadic actions depended primarily on the will and interests of powerful European states. Similarly, minority treaties that were incorporated in World War I peace settlements involved the protection of ethnic and religious minorities often related to or affiliated with the victorious powers. This undermined the credibility of international action for the protection of human rights. Moreover, many of these actions advanced a limited range of group rights and only indirectly contributed to the protection of individual rights.

It took a combination of events, personalities, and institutions to bring changes in the traditional Westphalian concept of national sovereignty and its effect on the protection of human rights in post-World War II Western Europe. For the first time, individuals became subjects of international law. This transcended traditional notions of national sovereignty under which the protection of human rights was in the exclusive domain of domestic jurisdiction. Until then, only states were subjects of international law. This important change in legal theory and diplomatic and political practice introduced a new era in the protection and promotion of human rights in Western Europe.

These changes were the result of many factors, including:

- the contributions of influential thinkers and actors as Eleanor Roosevelt, Charles Malik, Rene Cassin, and many others.
- the impact of World War II and the subsequent judgments in Nuremberg and Tokyo. This experiential process strengthened the commitment and moral argument of human rights advocates who sought changes in the traditional concept of sovereignty in order to advance the international protection of human rights.
- the expression and advocacy of this new thinking in human rights by regional and other international organizations in the post-World War II period. However controversial the presence of large numbers of newly independent states may have been in the UN General Assembly starting in the decade of the 1960s, it had a significant influence in the formulation and adoption of human rights covenants. The human rights debates in the UN General Assembly and in other UN organs also had a socializing and educational role not only for many of the new members of the UN but also for the traditional state members. It became a means of pressure on the older traditional members of these organizations to bring their human rights philosophies and practices closer to the views of the post-World War II international system. The end of

the Cold War lowered the political overtones of the human rights debate and increased its political credibility. The United States had traditionally avoided precise international legal obligations in the area of human rights on the grounds that politically motivated actions by Eastern bloc and third world countries could harm American interests and American citizens. Unfortunately, this attitude has not changed after the end of the Cold War. The United States exerted major diplomatic efforts to gain exceptions for U.S. citizens in the ratification of the statute of the International Criminal Court.

* the role of NGOs and other international networks. Their independent actions and investigations have kept governments "honest," have provided independent voices in the protection and enforcement of human rights, and have become one more means of pressure on governments reluctant to comply with current human rights standards.

This notable but gradual change to traditional notions of national sovereignty was not easily achieved. One classic work recognized that, despite its legal mandate, the European Commission of Human Rights moved cautiously in its early years.[7] This was necessary until it acquired the necessary confidence of the governments of members of the Council of Europe.

Thus, as another scholar has also stated, the worldwide prominence given to human rights today is one of the most remarkable developments of the post-World War II era. Human rights have finally "come in from the cold."[8] Despite the progress noted, there is no time for celebration. This study testifies to the existing gap between legal theory and political practice, and of the clashing priorities facing members of the international community when confronted with choices between economic and security interests and the protection of human rights. This theme will be developed further in the discussion of the implementation of rulings of the European Court of Human Rights and of the European Commission of Human Rights in the case of Cyprus.

Human Rights in the European Context

Cultural and political affinity, along with the impact of the consequences of World War II on the Western European psyche, provided momentum to European political and economic unification. It also became the impetus for the creation of major institutions for the protection of individual human rights with enforcement mechanisms transcending traditional notions of domestic jurisdiction. The institutional and procedural framework that emerged in Western Europe on 5 May 1949 with the creation of the Council of Europe, and in 1950 with the adoption of the European Convention of Human Rights, broke new ground in the promotion and protection of human rights. This unprecedented convention came into force in 1953.

The European Convention of Human Rights incorporated and elaborated in treaty form on most of the principles of the UN's Universal Declaration of Human Rights (1948). The European Convention also established appropriate institutional and procedural mechanisms for the implementation and enforcement of the rights guaranteed by the convention. The convention was supplemented by various protocols of equally binding validity, most important for our discussion being Protocol I (1954), which includes provisions on property rights, free elections, education, etc., and Protocol IV (1968) on personal liberties, freedom of movement, freedom from discrimination, etc. Furthermore, the members of the Council of Europe adopted numerous treaties complementing and elaborating on the principles of the European Convention and its protocols, including the European Social Charter (1965), the European Convention on the Prevention of Torture, Inhuman and Degrading Treatment or Punishment (1989), and various conventions on national minorities and their languages (1998).

The creation of the Council of Europe marked a major breakthrough in the international promotion and protection of human rights because members committed themselves to the rule of law and to the enjoyment of fundamental rights and freedoms. Those systematically violating these principles could be requested to withdraw or even be expelled, following a decision by the Committee of Ministers. This did happen in December 1969 when Greece withdrew from the Council of Europe rather than face expulsion or suspension for its apparent violations of the convention.[9]

There were various innovations introduced by the Council of Europe in the promotion and protection of human rights. These innovations were institutional as well as procedural. On the institutional side, the council created the European Commission of Human Rights and the European Court of Human Rights (1959) to which states and individuals had recourse under certain conditions. This two-tier system was replaced on 1 November 1998 by a full-time European Court of Human Rights, following the ratification of Protocol 11 of the convention by the members of the Council of Europe. After more than thirty years of work, the European Commission of Human Rights ceased to function and its cases were transferred to the European Court of Human Rights. This was one more example of the cautious institutional evolution in the area of human rights and of the political sensitivity that guided the intrusion into one of the traditional areas of sovereignty. In 1999, the council's institutional framework was expanded to include a High Commissioner of Human Rights, a position not only reflecting the importance assigned to human rights in Europe but also a position that paralleled the UN's and the OSCE's framework.

The original convention system introduced two new procedures for the protection of human rights. The first was under Article 24, where members could bring an application against another state member alleging violations of the European Convention. The second was the procedure of individual appeal under Article 25 of the convention. These procedures will be summarized because of their direct relevance to the issue of Cyprus.

Interstate applications are an indication of the collective interest of state members for the protection of human rights under the terms of the convention. Interstate cases have both a political and a legal character. The states filing such applications have determined not only that violations of the convention have occurred by another member but also that traditional diplomatic and political methods have not remedied the situation. Some have been critical of this procedure, especially when legal issues are overlaid by political ones.[10]

Under the original system, the commission examined the admissibility of a case and established the facts and, under a friendly settlement procedure, an attempt was made to remedy violations by mutual agreement. If that failed, the commission's opinion on whether a breach of the convention had occurred was forwarded to the Committee of Ministers which could either make a final decision or forward the case to the European Court of Human Rights. While the commission acted in a quasi-judicial manner, the Committee of Ministers that held the implementation power acted in a purely political manner. The commission performed remarkably well, as it had to overcome political pressures and the occasional noncooperation of a respondent state, as in the case of the applications filed against Turkey. It should be noted that the Committee of Ministers consisted of the foreign ministers (or their deputies) of the members of the Council of Europe. They were none else than the same ministers representing their countries in other collective security or economic organizations as the United Nations, the European Union/EEC, and NATO. These potentially conflicting roles highlighted the clash in the policy priorities of states and their membership obligations in various international and regional organizations. These organizations have different commitments to the "European Ideal" and are in different stages of development regarding the international protection of human rights. The priority given to human rights by the European Commission of Human Rights and the European Court of Human Rights is often in conflict with the political, security, and economic priorities of European Ministers of Foreign Affairs. Thus, on 28 May 1948 the International Court of Justice issued an advisory opinion endorsed by legal experts that political organs must act according to the conditions of a treaty, not political expediency. Unfortunately, the subordination of human rights to political, economic, and security considerations continues.

In the cases involving individual appeals (Article 25 of the original convention), the consent of the member state was also required. In turn, member states agreed to accept the court's jurisdiction. Since Protocol 11 to the convention came into effect in 1998, the consent of the home state is not required in individual appeals to the European Court of Human Rights. The applicant is required to have exhausted all available domestic remedies. Because of the heavy workload of the European Court of Human Rights, procedures have been introduced for hearing cases, whether in a committee of three judges, a chamber of seven judges, or a plenary session of seventeen judges. The enforcement of the decisions still remains in the hands of the Committee of Ministers.

In its first fifty years, the Council of Europe handled twenty interstate applications.[11] Ten of these applications involve Turkey, while six involve Cyprus from both the colonial and the post-colonial phase of the problem. Two of the cases on Cyprus involved[12] violations of the convention by Great Britain during the Greek Cypriot anti-colonial struggle, while four cases arose from Turkey's conduct during and since the 1974 Turkish invasion of Cyprus. The only case of noncompliance with decisions of the European Commission of Human Rights and the European Court of Human Rights on interstate applications involves the government of Turkey. The high rate of compliance with such decisions is an indicator of the legitimacy that institutions and procedures under the convention have attained in the last five decades. While Turkey remains the "odd ball" in this situation, its noncompliance points to the weaknesses identified earlier about the role of the Committee of Ministers. Implementation remains a political act, reflecting the reality that human rights may still have a secondary place when in conflict with security, economic, or other major political considerations.

Even a defiant state like Turkey is finding it increasingly difficult to justify its noncompliance. Turkey aspires to EU membership and resolutions by the Council of Ministers calling on Turkey to correct its behavior are a major embarrassment. The prospect of EU membership has now become an additional unanticipated enforcement mechanism of European Court decisions.

Despite the relative weakness in the enforcement in European Court of Human Rights decisions, the progress over the last five decades in the institutional and procedural protection of human rights under the Council of Europe is undeniable. It is anticipated that since the adoption of Protocol 11 to the European Convention, interstate cases are likely to decline, especially because individual appeals have been freed from prior restrictions other than the exhaustion of domestic remedies.

The impact of decisions of the European Court of Human Rights and the EU's European Court of Justice is significant for another reason, namely, the little-noticed adaptation of domestic legislation to European law, which is an aspect of European integration. Thus, in the emerging body of European jurisprudence, decisions by the European Court of Human Rights and the European Court of Justice are precedent-setting, requiring the adaptation of laws and court decisions of member states.[13] This is unprecedented in the history of the international protection and promotion of human rights.

The Emergence of a European Human Rights Regime

Two other major European institutions complement the human rights regime that started with the creation of the Council of Europe. Even though different in function and origins, the institutions of the European Union and of the Organization of Security and Cooperation in Europe complement and enhance those of the Council of Europe. All together, in the post-Cold War period, these institutions have contributed to the emergence of a European human rights regime unrivaled in any other part of the world.[14] This regime is based on common values, rules, complementary procedures, and institutions whose actions now have political and legal validity.

The end of the Cold War brought about the convergence of the rule of law, democracy, and protection of human rights across Europe. These principles were manifested in the text of the fiftieth anniversary Berlin Declaration of 25 March 2007 on the signing of the Rome Treaties that created the institutions today known as the European Union. These principles are also at the core of Article VI of the Founding Treaty of the European Union (Amsterdam Treaty, 1999).

All twenty-seven members of the European Union are also members of the Council of Europe and signatories to the European Convention. In 2000, the European Union adopted its own "European Charter of Fundamental Rights," whose content reflects and complements the provisions of the European Convention of Human Rights and the European Social Charter. Some have been critical of the duplication of legal instruments and institutions between the European Union and the Council of Europe. The fact remains that while all EU members are members of the Council of Europe, the reverse is not true. The complementarity in legal instruments and institutions strengthens the protection and promotion of human rights, keeping in mind that each of the organizations performs a variety of functions above and beyond human rights.

The Founding Treaty of the original European Economic Community at first had little direct reference to human rights. The EEC/EU relied on the formal commitment of its members to the European Convention of Human Rights. The institutionalization of the EU in 1999 required the formal adoption of an EU human rights regime which has given coherence to the priority assigned to human rights by the EU. The European Commission, the Council of Ministers, the European Parliament, and the European Commissioner of Human Rights each perform important monitoring roles in the field of human rights. In turn, the European Court of Justice has expanded its role in the area of human rights. It not only is an interpreter of law but is assuming the function of a constitutional court, especially in areas of property law and employment rights.[15]

The human rights monitoring role of various EU organs is reinforced by various powers ranging from hearings, quiet diplomacy, the threat of sanctions, revocation of voting rights, and even the suspension of membership in extreme cases.[16] One new element in the creation of a European human rights regime is the fact that prospective EU members must meet clearly defined human rights standards under the EU's Copenhagen membership criteria. The criteria are now part of the EU Founding Treaty. Thus, EU enlargement is now conditioned on the respect of human rights, democracy, and the rule of law, and on the strict convergence of domestic laws to instruments like the European Convention and the EU's Charter of Fundamental Rights. This has been one of the major issues in Turkey's difficulties as it sought EU candidate status and, later, a date for the commencement of accession talks. The accession talks that commenced in the fall of 2005 between Turkey and the EU have run into various difficulties, including the implementation of many human rights rules in Turkish domestic law.

Thus, EU enlargement is now conditioned on the respect of human rights, democracy, and the rule of law broadly defined. This conditionality has been very important in bringing about institutional, legal, and procedural changes in the domestic policies of prospective members. This is an unprecedented new tool in the protection and promotion of human rights on the European continent. On 1 March 2007, the EU also established the EU

Fundamental Rights Agency, an instrument designed to combat discrimination, racism, xenophobia, and intolerance.

In the middle of the Cold War and after long negotiations, the Conference on Security and Cooperation in Europe (CSCE) drafted and adopted in 1975 what came to be known as the Helsinki Final Act. After the end of the Cold War in 1992, the conference transformed itself into the Organization on Security and Cooperation in Europe (OSCE). The 1975 Helsinki Final Act included three "baskets," the first of which guaranteed the inviolability of European frontiers and upheld the sovereignty, equality, and territorial integrity of states. In the "human dimension" (Principle 7) section it included lengthy explanatory paragraphs on the CSCE's commitment to human rights issues. In contrast to the Council of Europe and the EU, the human rights commitments of CSCE/OSCE members were more in the form of encouragement rather than a binding enforceable commitment. This is explained partially by the fact that the OSCE was primarily a political organization not founded on a treaty. Thus, even though the OSCE has a most detailed human rights regime, borrowing much from the UN and other European human rights instruments, it has limited legal sanction for noncompliance. Its power is based on political persuasion and consensus because of its diverse and expansive membership. Thus, OSCE commitments are binding but without the force of law. The inclusion of major powers in the OSCE such as Russia and the United States has also undermined OSCE effectiveness. This is why the organization has limited political capacity to intervene in the affairs of major members.

Following the end of the Cold War, the linkage of human rights, democracy, and the rule of law became the foundation of the OSCE. This has been an important development tool for newer members of the international system from the Balkans and the former Soviet Union. Even though the OSCE has been ineffective in moderating Russian conduct in Chechnya, OSCE monitoring missions have become an important means in the protection of human rights in the Balkans and Central Asia. Countries of these regions are now developing a human rights regime that parallels that of the rest of the European continent.

Thus, the evolving European human rights regime has had a major impact on the promotion and protection of human rights. The combined force of moral persuasion, sanctions, and formal commitments has transformed the promotion and protection of human rights in a manner unthinkable to the pioneers that drafted the UDHR nearly sixty years ago.

CHAPTER THREE

Cyprus and the European Human Rights Institutions

CYPRUS became an independent state on 16 August 1960. A month later, the Republic of Cyprus joined the United Nations. The treaty establishing the Republic of Cyprus (Article 5) provided that Cypriots would enjoy rights and freedoms comparable to those under the European Convention and its Protocol I. On 24 May 1961, Cyprus formally acceded to the treaty creating the Council of Europe, becoming its sixteenth member. In 1972 the Republic of Cyprus entered into an Economic Association Agreement with the European Economic Community which was to be expanded to a Customs Union Agreement over a ten-year period. In 1990, Cyprus applied for membership in the EEC/EC. The Cypriot application was accepted in 1994 and accession negotiations opened in 1998. On 16 April 2003, the Republic of Cyprus signed the Treaty of Accession to the European Union (formerly the EEC/EC) and assumed its membership in that organization on 1 May 2004.

By its signature to the Treaty of Accession, Cyprus committed itself to the principles guiding the EU and to the Charter of Fundamental Rights (2000) of the European Union. As shown in chapter two, in addition to the economic and political objectives, EU accession carried with it major commitments to human rights, democracy, and the rule of law (Article VI of the EU Founding Treaty).

The Republic of Cyprus also participated in the Conference on Security and Cooperation in Europe and signed the documents of the Helsinki Final Act on 1 August 1975. Cyprus became a member to the successor of the conference, the Organization for Security and Cooperation in Europe. On 6 October 2005, the Parliament of the Republic of Cyprus ratified the proposed European Constitution, which is currently in limbo following its rejection in the referenda held in France and the Netherlands in 2005.[1]

By joining these institutions, signing the Helsinki Final Act, and ratifying the proposed European Constitution, Cyprus made a major formal commitment to the international promotion and protection of human rights and to the emerging European human rights regime. These actions reflected the values that have guided the Republic of Cyprus since independence and its commitment to the European economic, social, and political space.

The Republic of Cyprus became the victim of the 1974 Turkish invasion, continuing occupation, and massive continuing violations of internationally guaranteed human rights by the occupation forces. Therefore, it was not surprising for Cyprus to turn to the European human rights institutional and procedural framework to protect its interests and to remedy the consequences of the Turkish invasion. Turkey, too, was a signatory to the European Convention of Human Rights and the Helsinki Final Act, among other relevant international treaties. The implications of this will be discussed throughout this volume. Cypriot legal and legislative institutions, like those of the other members of these European institutions, continue the process of adaptation to the requirements of the transnational legal obligations of the republic. This is an ongoing process, as European-wide laws and court decisions must be applied at the micro level, not only at the macro level.[2]

Precedents and Lessons

Cyprus was not a newcomer to the European Convention. It first came under the convention's terms[3] on 23 October 1953, when Great Britain extended the convention to this colonial territory. A state of emergency was declared on Cyprus by the colonial authorities on 7 October 1955, following the Greek Cypriot anticolonial rebellion that had started a few months earlier. Because of these conditions, on 13 April 1956 Great Britain informed the secretary-general of the Council of Europe that it would apply derogations from the European Convention in the case of Cyprus. On 7 May 1956, Greece, a member of the Council of Europe, filed an interstate application against Great Britain in the European Commission of Human Rights alleging that the exceptional measures applied by the colonial authorities in Cyprus violated the European Convention of Human Rights. A second interstate application was also lodged on 17 July 1957, containing forty-nine cases of torture and ill treatment of Greek Cypriot detainees by British authorities. The European Commission of Human Rights[4] declared both cases admissible, although twenty of the forty-nine cases in the second application were not included on the grounds that domestic remedies had not been exhausted.

The Greek move against Great Britain was primarily intended to protect Greek Cypriots from the abusive practices of the colonial authorities. Chapter two noted that interstate applications served political objectives in addition to enforcing human rights standards. Interstate applications were a tool to elicit international pressure to resolve an interstate dispute after failure to resolve it or to remedy convention violations by diplomatic means. The cases filed by Greece against Great Britain were a classic example. However, they were also within the spirit and the intent of the procedures included in the European Convention.

On 2 October 1958, the Sub-Commission of the European Commission of Human Rights charged with establishing the facts and seeking a friendly settlement sent its report on the first application to the Committee of Ministers of the Council of Europe, while continuing its investigation of the second Greek interstate application. The outcome of both applications was overtaken by events. Greece, Great Britain, and Turkey concluded the London Agreement of 19 February 1959 which gave independence to Cyprus. On 20 August 1959, the Committee of Ministers of the Council of Europe accepted a joint request by Greece and Great Britain that no further action was needed in these two interstate applications as the London Agreement resolved the dispute over Cyprus.

These two interstate applications were the first to test the system created under the convention. These precedent-setting cases established procedures and standards next to be applied in the Austrian complaint against Italy in 1960.

The outcome of the first two interstate applications handled by the European Commission of Human Rights was deficient for two reasons. First, it undermined the friendly settlement procedure of the convention (original Article 28) and avoided the issue of remedies for established violations of the convention. The cases were closed by mutual agreement of the parties. The report of the European Commission of Human Rights was sealed until the late 1990s, nearly forty years after the fact. This spared Great Britain from the political embarrassment of violations documented in the report, without contributing to the protection of human rights under the convention. Second, the protection of human rights was linked to the tripartite political settlement reached in London, while no measures were taken against Great Britain for its actual violations of the convention that occurred in Cyprus during the anticolonial rebellion.

It should be noted that former UN Secretary-General Kofi Annan, in the fifth version of his 2004 arbitration plan on Cyprus, attempted a similar political maneuver. The secretary-general's attempted action failed because of the rejection of his arbitration plan by Greek Cypriot voters in the referendum of 24 April 2004. Had Annan V been approved by the referenda held in both communities, all the legal cases brought by Greek Cypriots against Turkey and pending at the European Court of Human Rights would have been withdrawn by a request of the government of the new Cypriot republic that would have been created under Annan V. This would have been done by government action without the approval of the applicants. Had this occurred, it would have been a significant blow to the credibility of the convention and of the European Court of Human Rights. An arbitrated political settlement, approved by simultaneous and separate referenda in each of the two communities, would have taken precedence over pending court actions in cases filed by Cypriot nationals in the European Court of Human Rights against Turkey. Annan V would also have deprived all Cypriot citizens of legal rights under the convention. These court cases would have been politically and financially damaging to Turkey. As the discussion below will show, Turkey had already been found guilty of serious violations of the convention in four Cypriot interstate applications and in a number of court cases brought by individual Cypriots against Turkey in the European Court of Human Rights. Precedents set by these cases and the rationale that guided the legal decisions of the European Court of Human Rights were a good indicator of rulings to come in the cases pending in the European Court against Turkey. This was especially true in property cases pending against Turkey. Greek Cypriot property owners had been deprived of access to and enjoyment of their properties by the occupation authorities since the 1974 Turkish invasion. Moreover, the occupied areas of Cyprus had been ethnically cleansed while the occupation authorities had issued false titles for usurped Greek Cypriot property to Turkish Cypriots, Turkish settlers, and other foreign nationals. These usurped properties had been illegally sold for substantial profit.

The European Court of Human Rights addressed property issues in the context of the European Convention and international law. In contrast, Kofi Annan's 2004 arbitration plan on Cyprus violated the European Convention in the case of the properties of the displaced and the refugees. This is why Turkey and its allies insisted on having the cases pending in the European Court of Human Rights withdrawn. Annan's arbitration plan would have taken precedence over European law. A political agreement would have affected not only cases pending in the European Court of Human Rights but also potential future cases arising from the implementation of his arbitration plan. This would have deprived all Cypriot citizens of fundamental rights under the European Convention. This arbitration plan was one more example of the settlement-at-any-cost approach in resolving the Cyprus problem. It is ironic that the UN secretary-general, the guardian of the treaties deposited with the United Nations, was willing to propose solutions violating those treaties and the rule of law.

Politics and Human Rights

U.S. and UN mediators on Cyprus placed political and security interests above human rights and considered the protection of human rights dependent on a political settlement. This is why no remedies were provided for the documented violations of human rights in Cyprus during and since the 1974 Turkish invasion. Turkey and its allies considered such remedies as an obstacle to talks leading to a settlement rather than as a means to a settlement. Two examples will suffice. The White House lobbied hard in the U.S. Congress in 1974 and 1975 not to punish Turkey for its invasion of Cyprus by suspending military aid under the terms of the U.S. Military Assistance Act. The lobbying continued during the congressionally mandated arms embargo until it was lifted in 1978. The White House argued that sanctions hindered the political settlement and undermined U.S. regional security interests.

The second example involves lobbying directed by the United States, not a member of the Council of Europe, and by Great Britain toward the Committee of Ministers of the Council of Europe. The Committee of Ministers had the authority to act on the reports of the European Commission of Human Rights involving violations of the European Convention by member states. U.S. and British lobbying efforts sought to avoid the imposition of any sanctions on Turkey for the violations of the European Convention documented by the European Commission of Human Rights. The United States and Great Britain also sought to keep secret reports by the European Commission on Human Rights on the Cypriot interstate applications against Turkey. Once more, the United States argued that sanctions and negative publicity would undermine both Western security at a time of growing East-West tensions and relations with and the stability of a Western ally (that is, Turkey) and would hinder talks on the resolution of the Cyprus problem. Both the United States and Great Britain saw the restoration of human rights as an outcome of a political settlement and not as a means to a political settlement.

Anglo-American lobbying proved successful. On 21 October 1977, responding to the report on the first two Cypriot interstate applications, the Committee of Ministers concluded:

> Certain events which occurred in Cyprus constitute violations of the European Convention for the Protection of Human Rights. Consequently, it asks that measures be taken in order to put an end to such violations as might continue to occur and so that such events are not repeated.

The Committee of Ministers went a step further and argued that

> the enduring protection of human rights in Cyprus calls for the re-establishment of peace and confidence between the two communities on the island. Therefore, it strongly urged the parties to resume inter-communal talks with the minimum delay.[5]

The committee decided to wait at least nine months to take up the matter again and decided to keep the commission's report secret.

The commission's report had leaked to the press by January 1977, creating a major political embarrassment for the Council of Ministers and for Turkey in particular. The nine-month time limit may have been within the Committee of Ministers mandate but it nevertheless was excessive, given that almost four years had gone by since the submission of the first Cypriot interstate application while the violations of human rights in Cyprus continued. After repeated politically motivated delays, the Committee of Ministers declassified the report and the related documentation on 31 August 1979, while calling on the parties to engage in intercommunal talks in the interest of the enduring protection of human rights. Regrettably, this decision sidestepped the issue of the Turkish invasion and its consequences and reduced the Cyprus problem to an intercommunal problem in need of resolution. A political body had made a political decision. It showed greater sensitivity to American and UN negotiating initiatives[6] than the need to remedy the violations of the European Convention documented by the European Commission of Human Rights. Needless to say, no progress was achieved in the absence of substantive pressure on Turkey.

Similar was the fate of the report on the third Cypriot interstate application against Turkey (8007/77) that addressed continuous violations of human rights by Turkey in Cyprus. The commission's report, adopted on 4 October 1983, found Turkey in violation of several articles of the European Convention and of Protocol I. Moreover, the commission determined that remedies proposed by Turkey were neither relevant nor sufficient, and that these violations were directed against Greek Cypriots because of their ethnic origin, race, and religion. This was in direct violation of Article 14 of the convention. The Committee of Ministers made this report public on 2 April 1992, more than eleven years after its adoption by the commission, without taking any steps against Turkey for violations documented seriatim in all three interstate applications.

The experience with the first three Cypriot interstate applications clearly shows the conflict between the obligations of member states of the Council of Europe in cases involving human rights in interstate disputes. This conflict undermined the effectiveness of appropriate quasi-judicial actions at the European Commission of Human Rights. While the commission functioned properly within its mandate, the Committee of Ministers gave precedence to political and security considerations over human rights. The Committee of Ministers' reasoning did not contribute to the resolution of the Cyprus problem. By avoiding the issue of the Turkish invasion and continuing occupation of Cyprus, the ministers undermined the cause of human rights.

The outcome of the fourth interstate application filed by the Republic of Cyprus in 1994 against Turkey[7] is more encouraging. On 10 May 2001, the European Court of Human Rights delivered a wide-ranging decision that addressed in depth the legal consequences of Turkey's invasion and continuing occupation of Cyprus under contemporary international law. The decision also addressed humanitarian issues involving the missing, the properties of refugees and displaced persons, and the living conditions of the enclaved. In all these areas, Turkey was found in serious violation of the European Convention. In contrast to the first three Cypriot interstate applications, the court's decision became public immediately. This was an indication that the members of the Council of Europe had lost patience with Turkey's intransigence and with the Committee of Ministers' reluctance to take measures to enforce decisions documenting Turkey's violations of the convention. This was also evidenced by resolutions adopted by the Parliamentary Assembly of the Council of Europe calling for Turkey's compliance with court rulings and calling on the Council of Ministers to "take all necessary measures to ensure the execution of the Court's decisions without delay."[8] After 2001, the Committee of Ministers felt the growing political pressure generated by resolutions and recommendations of the Parliamentary Assembly of the Council of Europe. Turkey's continued defiance of European Court rulings in the Loizidou case was an additional embarrassment to the Committee of Ministers at a time when Turkey sought accession talks with the European Union. In a series of decisions starting in 2001, the Committee of Ministers began calling on Turkey to implement the European Court of Human Rights decision in the precedent-setting Loizidou case and reminded Turkey of its obligations and commitments under the European Convention.

As shown, the Committee of Ministers had been reluctant to impose sanctions on Turkey. However, the repeated findings by the European Commission of Human Rights, the European Court of Human Rights, the Parliamentary Assembly of the Council of Europe, and Turkey's interest in becoming a EU member forced the issue of the implementation of the decisions on Turkey's violations of human rights in Cyprus. Turkey could not continue to defy the European legal order and expect that its EU accession path would continue unhindered. This is an encouraging development, pointing once more to the cautious progress in the protection of human rights in post-World War II Europe. It also shows how complementary actions under the European human rights regime can bring about compliance on the rare occasion of defiant behavior by a European state. Because Turkey sought accession talks with the EU, it was compelled to pay Titina Loizidou the compensation and penalties imposed by the European Court of Human Rights for the loss of use and enjoyment of her property in the occupied city of Kyrenia. Until then, Turkey had defied the court ruling.

The thesis of this study is that the restoration and protection of human rights in Cyprus is independent of the political settlement of the problem and must not wait for such a settlement. The restoration and protection of human rights should be the foundation of a viable and functional settlement, one that allows Cyprus to meet its international and EU obligations.

Human Rights and the Solution to the Cyprus Problem

Human rights issues were introduced in the European legal and political agenda in the mid-1950s by the colonial phase of the Cyprus problem, long before the prominence given to human rights in post-Cold War Europe. The 1974 Turkish invasion of Cyprus has caused major documented human rights violations that continue to this day. Cyprus has become a major testing ground of the priority given to the rule of law, democracy, and human rights in post-Cold War Europe.

There are several reasons for this. First, the Republic of Cyprus is a member of the European Union, while Turkey commenced accession negotiations with the European Union in September of 2005. Despite these developments, Turkey continues to occupy nearly 37 percent of the territory of an EU member and does not recognize the Republic of Cyprus or its government. Instead, it recognizes the authorities of the secessionist entity it created in occupied Cyprus in 1983. Turkey is also in defiance of decisions of the European Court of Human Rights. Both actions violate basic legal conventions that are at the heart of the European human rights regime. Turkey is a party to these conventions. As an applicant for EU membership, Turkey is also in violation of principles included in Article VI of the Founding Treaty of the EU.[9] Turkish compliance with European human rights standards in the case of Cyprus and the implementation of the required changes in Turkey's domestic laws would remove some of the major obstacles in Turkey's road to Brussels. Second, the presence of an effective framework of European human rights legislation and institutions to which Turkey is a party has removed one of the key obstacles that confronted the UN-sponsored talks on the resolution of the Cyprus problem. Turkey's guarantee and military presence on the island would not be needed to protect Turkish Cypriot rights, as Turkey and some of its allies have argued in the past. Turkish Cypriots, as EU citizens in a reunited Cyprus, would enjoy the full range of rights and protections available to all EU citizens.

Third, the human rights issues that will be analyzed in this volume are the very essence of the Cyprus problem. Since the accession of Cyprus to the EU, these issues can be resolved in the context of the European human rights regime outlined earlier. Thus, remedying the violations of human rights issues will provide the foundation of a viable and functional political settlement and will remove one of the major obstacles to Turkey's EU candidacy.

Turkey, along with the United States and Great Britain, has consistently argued that only a political settlement can guarantee the restoration and protection of human rights. They have opposed any sanctions against Turkey for violations of human rights covenants that occurred during and since the 1974 invasion. They have also opposed legal actions at and by European human rights institutions on the grounds that such actions are obstacles to a political settlement through intercommunal talks. The most effective response to this point has come from the European Court of Human Rights in the fourth Cypriot interstate application against Turkey (2001). The European Court has found that ongoing intercommunal talks cannot legitimize convention violations or become an excuse for not remedying these violations.

The Anglo-American position that only a political settlement can guarantee the restoration and protection of human rights merits further discussion because it is based on a circular argument. Human rights violations in Cyprus are considered to be the result of a local political conflict, rather than the result of the Turkish invasion and continuing occupation. Consequently, only a political settlement can assure the nonrecurrence of these violations. This simplistic thesis leads to another conclusion. If the Cyprus problem is only an intercommunal problem and not a problem of invasion, continuing occupation, and violation of internationally recognized human rights, ethnic separation is one way of resolving it. Ethnic separation has been the aim of Turkish policy since 1955. This type of simplistic thinking finds precedent in the U.S. actions in the Balkans following the collapse of former Yugoslavia. Certain NGOs have also adopted similar thinking for problems in the Balkans and have even proposed border changes under the guise of protecting human rights. Such simplistic answers legitimize ethnic cleansing and potentially contribute to regional instability.

The situation in the Balkans is a dangerous precedent for Cyprus. By reducing the Cyprus problem to an intercommunal problem, Turkey and its allies deliberately avoid addressing the fact that the Cyprus problem was and remains one of invasion and continuing occupation. This is why the restoration of human rights and appropriate remedies for such violations can become the foundation of a viable political settlement in conformity with European law. It is the lack of sanctions that has encouraged Turkey's negotiating intransigence on Cyprus and undermined the effectiveness of the European human rights regime. Past and continuing violations of human rights in Cyprus have not been remedied. Instead, the impetus given to political solutions violating fundamental principles of European human rights law has contributed to the continuation of Turkey's human rights violations on the island. The arbitration settlement proposed by former UN secretary-general Kofi Annan in 2004 remains a classic example of this political approach.

Critics of introducing human rights in the search for a solution to the Cyprus problem have advanced various arguments, all of which let Turkey "off the hook," so to speak, for its past and continuing violations of human rights in Cyprus. One typical argument is that raising human rights issues and related court actions creates obstacles to an effective political solution by embarrassing Turkey. On the contrary, actions contributing to the restoration of human rights and conforming with international and European law give legitimacy to a political settlement.

The same critics argue that politicizing human rights impoverishes the cause of human rights and reduces the chances of a political compromise. On the contrary, downgrading human rights weakens the legitimacy of any political solution in the eyes of those who have to live under its terms. This was one of the reasons for the Greek Cypriot rejection of Kofi Annan's fifth version of his 2004 arbitration plan on Cyprus. Acceptance of that plan would have made all Cypriots second-class citizens in their own country by depriving them of fundamental rights enjoyed by all other EU citizens. This study will show that the Cypriot grievances are real, documented, and continuing. There can be no compromise in implementing fundamental principles of the European Convention and other instruments that make up the European human rights regime. Compromise in the name of political expediency would destroy the progress made in the protection of human rights in Europe over the last half century, and would not advance the cause of the reunification of Cyprus.

A second argument often heard in the case of Cyprus is the obsolescence of the problem. Advocates of this position consider the events of 1974 to be regrettable. However, they also claim that because these events took place more than three decades ago, they have been superseded by other, more pressing, international problems affecting human rights and political, economic, and security interests. Because of the current conditions in Turkey and the eastern Mediterranean and the Middle East, Turkey's advocates call for sensitivity rather than sanctions in dealing with Turkey. The response to this argument is clear and unequivocal. The protection of human rights and the implementation of provisions of international and European law, agreed to by Turkey, are not dependent on the state of Turkey's domestic politics or the stability of Turkey's regional political environment. There is no statute of limitations on Turkey's misconduct in Cyprus. Turkey's documented violations of human rights are not limited to the events surrounding the 1974 invasion of Cyprus. Turkey's violations of European and international law continue at this time. One of the key reasons for the perpetuation of the Cyprus problem has been Turkey's intransigence that can be attributed to the support extended to Turkey primarily by the United States. Washington continues to place security and political and economic considerations above the restoration and protection of human rights in Cyprus. Had the proper emphasis been given to the implementation of the decisions of the European Commission of Human Rights in the first three Cypriot interstate applications, we would not be faced today with the current stalemate. As long as Turkey continues to rely on such external support, its violations of European and international law will continue in the absence of sanctions and remedies for these violations. Thus, political expediency has undermined the effectiveness of the European human rights regime and the prospects for a viable political settlement. The problem is not with the quasi-judicial or judicial mechanisms of the Council of Europe but with its chief political organ, the Committee of Ministers, that is charged with the implementation of the judicial decisions. This body has been willing to subordinate human rights to political, security, and economic considerations. Speaking to the issue of political expediency, the International Court of Justice in a 1948 Advisory Opinion[10] ruled that political organs must act according to the conditions of a treaty and not according to political expediency.

The issue of human rights in primarily political disputes merits further discussion. The Cyprus problem, like other international disputes, is characterized by an interplay of legal and political issues in the definition of the policies of the parties involved in the dispute. There is no doubt that, in the aftermath of the Turkish invasion, Cyprus, a small and weak state and victim of external aggression, relied on legal principles. This was done in order to protect Cypriot sovereignty, territorial integrity, and independence and the rights of the victims of Turkey's aggression. Small states typically rely on legal arguments to enhance their political claims when confronted by a stronger power with powerful allies. In the case of the continuing and documented violations of human rights by Turkey in Cyprus, framing key issues in the context of the European human rights regime allowed the government of Cyprus to seize the high moral ground in this perpetuated dispute. Given the failure of international initiatives to resolve the Cyprus problem,[11] resort to international organizations and to the organs of the Council of Europe was and remains an important part of the strategy of internationalization of the Cyprus problem. This did not impoverish human rights. On the contrary, it elevated the importance of human rights issues in the search for a viable solution of the Cyprus problem and made human rights the foundation of any future settlement. Remedies available under international law were important not only for the protection of human rights but also for sending a message to Turkey that its continuing misconduct could not be tolerated under the European human rights regime. The priority given to human rights in a legitimate liberation struggle was an appropriate weapon in the diplomatic arsenal of the Republic of Cyprus. Restoring the rights of all Cypriots, penalizing Turkey for its misconduct, ending the continuing violations of human rights in Cyprus, and using human rights as the foundation of a viable political settlement were legitimate acts. They were also within the intent of the instruments available in Europe for the protection and promotion of human rights.

In its examination of the third Cypriot interstate application against Turkey,[12] the European Commission of Human Rights found that this application did not misuse the convention, nor was it "in any sense abusive." This ruling was in response to Turkey's allegation that the repeated Cypriot applications to the European Commission of Human Rights were abusive and violated the spirit of the convention. The commission's ruling was one more affirmation of the importance of the interstate application process in the European human rights regime.

The Internationalization of the Cyprus Problem

The policy of the internationalization of the Cyprus problem was a multifaceted, dynamic policy combining bilateral and multilateral diplomatic actions with complementary and mutually reinforcing objectives. It involved actions in various organs of the United Nations and the various European regional organizations discussed in chapter two. It was a conscious political decision on the part of the government of a small and weak state that fell victim to the designs of a larger and more powerful neighbor supported by influential states. The objectives of the policy of internationalization were numerous and clear. The objectives listed below are not in any priority order:

- to expose and prevent the threatened partition of Cyprus;
- to uphold the independence, sovereignty, unity, and territorial integrity and the legitimacy of the Republic of Cyprus;
- to pressure Turkey into meaningful negotiations;
- to assure Turkey's compliance with the European Convention and its other international obligations;
- to redress the violations of human rights and seek measures for Turkey's noncompliance with the decisions of European and other institutions;
- to indirectly pressure Turkey's influential allies; and
- to safeguard the rights of all Cypriot citizens under relevant European conventions.

Some of these were aimed indirectly at the United States, Turkey's chief patron. Human rights were an important part of declaratory American foreign policy and in foreign and security policy legislation adopted by the U.S. Congress.[13] In the post-Vietnam period, the U.S. Congress had shown sensitivity to matters of law and human rights in U.S. foreign and security policy. Thus, pressure from Congress on the executive branch was expected to have a positive effect on American policy on Cyprus.

It is ironic that Cyprus, a victim of aggression and continuing occupation, has been criticized for politicizing human rights by states that have done so routinely in their foreign policy since the end of World War II. A classic example is the "Report on Human Rights Practices" for each of the countries of the world, other than the United States, published annually by the U.S. Department of State. This report is sent to appropriate committees of the U.S. House of Representatives and Senate. The selective reporting on human rights practices of friends and foes of the United States is striking, undermining the credibility of the report. A reading of the chapters involving Turkey and Cyprus absolves Turkey of its actions in Cyprus in and since 1974. The report does not account for any of the decisions by European human rights institutions in the case of Turkey's consistent and gross violations of human rights in Cyprus. Moreover, the United States, which is not a member of the Council of Europe or the European Union, has lobbied hard European foreign ministers not to impose sanctions on Turkey despite its documented violations of human rights in Cyprus. Nor does this report take into account the fact that Turkey has signed and ratified the major European human rights conventions. This is a classic example of the politicization of human rights and the subordination of human rights to political, security, and economic considerations. Similar is the case with the willingness of European foreign ministers to heed Washington's advice and avoid measures implementing decisions of European human rights institutions.

At the risk of sounding polemical, the time has come to avoid double standards and not to criticize countries that violate their obligations under international conventions. Such double standards have undermined the search for a viable solution to the Cyprus problem and the priority given to the rule of law, democracy, and human rights in post-Cold War Europe. Recent resolutions by the Parliamentary Assembly calling on the Committee of Ministers of the Council of Europe to address Turkey's defiance of European law are an encouraging sign.

Regional and International Institutions and the Protection of Human Rights in Cyprus

The policy of internationalization of the Cyprus problem involved resorting to international and regional organizations with the objective of protecting the sovereignty, territorial integrity, and independence of the Republic of Cyprus and the protection of the rights of all its citizens. This became necessary and urgent as the objectives of the Turkish invasion and continuing occupation became clear. Turkey aimed at the creation of two states in Cyprus under the guise of a loose confederation, and the dissolution of the internationally recognized Republic of Cyprus. This amounted to a legalized partition of Cyprus and to the legitimization of ethnic cleansing and of the other documented violations of human rights during and since 1974.

Turkey is a signatory of most major post-World War II international treaties that addressed issues of human rights directly or indirectly. These include, but are not limited to:

- the Charter of the United Nations;
- the Universal Declaration of Human Rights;
- the 1949 Geneva Conventions;
- the Statute of the Council of Europe;
- the European Convention of Human Rights;
- the Association Agreement with the EEC and the agreement governing Turkey's EU accession negotiations;
- the Helsinki Final Act; and
- all the major UN-sponsored treaties of the post-World War II period.

Various organs of the United Nations, the Council of Europe, and the European Union have adopted numerous resolutions on aspects of the Cyprus problem and have censured Turkey for its violations of human rights under contemporary international law.[14] This will be fully documented and analyzed in the chapters that follow.

Since 1974, the United Nations Security Council, the General Assembly, the Commission of Human Rights, and the Sub-Commission on the Prevention of Discrimination and Protection of Minorities have adopted resolutions which:

- uphold the sovereignty, unity, and territorial integrity of the Republic of Cyprus;
- recognize only the Republic of Cyprus and its government;
- call for the respect and for the restoration of human rights, including the freedom of movement, settlement, property ownership, and the voluntary return of displaced persons and refugees in safety;
- endorsed the principle that the force of arms does not influence the resolution of the Cyprus problem and have called for the withdrawal of "foreign" forces from Cyprus;
- recognize the plight of the refugees and the displaced and call for their safe and voluntary return to their homes;
- condemn secessionist activities in occupied Cyprus. Such actions have been declared illegal and invalid;
- condemn the presence of settlers from mainland Turkey and the attempted demographic changes in occupied Cyprus; and
- call for humanitarian actions concerning the missing persons in Cyprus.

The European Court of Human Rights, the European Commission of Human Rights, and the Parliamentary Assembly of the Council of Europe have documented and condemned specific violations of the European Convention by the Turkish occupation forces in Cyprus:

- They determined that ongoing intercommunal talks are no excuse for the continuing human rights violations or for the nonimplementation of Court and Commission decisions. Intercommunal talks do not legitimize convention violations.
- They upheld the legitimacy of the Republic of Cyprus and its government.
- They affirmed the illegality of the entity known as the "Turkish Republic of Northern Cyprus," which has been found to be a "subordinate local administration" to Turkey. The creation of this entity by the occupation army did not affect the continuing existence of the Republic of Cyprus. The Republic of Cyprus remains a single state.
- They determined that under international law, the so-called "TRNC" was not a state and was therefore illegal, and should not be recognized.
- They acknowledge that Turkey is in effective control of the occupied areas of Cyprus and therefore responsible for what happens in the occupied territory of Cyprus. If Turkey connives or acquiesces to private acts violating the convention, it is also responsible for such violations.
- They affirmed the right to property while documenting continuing violations of personal rights, the missing, and so on.

- Appeals by Cypriot displaced and refugees were accepted in the absence of effective local remedies in occupied Cyprus.
- They determined that actions taken against Greek Cypriots following the 1974 invasion constituted discrimination on the grounds of ethnicity, language and religion. Such discrimination is explicitly prohibited under the European Convention.

The institutions of the European Union, including the European Parliament:

- have upheld actions and decisions of the UN Security Council and of the Council of Europe;
- have stressed Turkey's obligation to comply with the *acquis communautaire* and with European law in order to make progress in its EU accession path;
- have condemned the creation of the "TRNC" in the occupied territories;
- have called for the withdrawal of Turkish troops and settlers. This is considered an important step for the normalization of relations between the EU and Turkey;
- have condemned the systematic destruction of the Greek Cypriot cultural heritage in occupied Cyprus;
- have condemned the murders in cold blood of Greek Cypriot demonstrators in the neutral zone in 1996 by Turkish forces and agents of the occupation regime; and
- agreed in 1999 that the Republic of Cyprus could become an EU member even without a solution of the Cyprus problem.

This brief summary of various international actions on Cyprus provides a framework for the discussion of the specific violations of human rights that have occurred and continue to occur in Cyprus. These summary comments should be read in conjunction with the analysis in chapter two about the European human rights institutions, and the fact that under Article 25 of the UN Charter, UN members are obligated to accept and carry out decisions of the Security Council. In the case of Cyprus, the Security Council has adopted more than ninety unanimous resolutions that remain unimplemented.

In Conclusion

The first three chapters of this study have provided a brief historical introduction to Cyprus and to the Cyprus problem. They have analyzed the evolution of the international protection of human rights and the emergence of a European human rights regime, along with its strengths and weaknesses. Finally, this chapter addressed the impact of the participation of the Republic of Cyprus in the European human rights regime and the implications for the resolution of the Cyprus problem. Despite the progress noted in the European institutional and procedural human rights framework, the conflict in the priorities of member states continues. This is why declaratory human rights statements often find no application and are subordinated to political, economic, and security considerations.

The remaining chapters are devoted to a detailed examination of the violations of European and international law committed by Turkey in Cyprus during and since 1974. The documented evidence will show that, contrary to the claims of Turkey and its allies, the Cyprus problem is not an intercommunal problem but a problem of invasion, continuing occupation, and documented violations of human rights that continue to this day. Only by bringing to an end the consequences of the Turkish invasion will a viable solution to the Cyprus problem be possible. Human rights, as defined and protected by the European human rights regime, remain the foundation of a viable and functional solution and not the other way around. Such a solution will allow the Republic of Cyprus to continue to meet its international obligations and will allow all Cypriot citizens to enjoy the rights of all other citizens of the EU.

CHAPTER FOUR

Invasion, Continuing Occupation, and Violations of Personal Rights

THE REMAINING chapters in this volume will present documented evidence of specific human rights violations committed by Turkey in Cyprus during and since the 1974 invasion. The evidence that will be presented explains why the Republic of Cyprus brought its case to European human rights institutions, why the restoration of human rights provides the foundation for a lasting settlement of the Cyprus problem, and why Cyprus became the testing ground of the rule of law, democracy, and human rights in post-Cold War Europe. The analysis will show that Turkey's actions were directed at Greek Cypriots because of their ethnicity, language, and religion.

The Turkish invasion commenced on 20 July 1974, a few days after a coup carried out against the legitimate government of the Republic of Cyprus by the junta ruling Greece at the time. Claiming to act under Article 4 of the Treaty of Guarantee, Turkey invaded the Republic of Cyprus to restore the status quo ante, that is, to restore the 1960 constitutional order. In an unprecedented air, naval, and ground assault, Turkey established a beachhead on the northern coast of Cyprus. It repeatedly violated the UN Security Council-imposed ceasefire in order to consolidate its military position on the island. Turkey attempted to use the UN-sponsored negotiations in Geneva to impose a settlement on Cyprus and to prepare for the second phase of its invasion that commenced on 14 August 1974. When the fighting was over, the U.S.-equipped Turkish forces prevailed over the small and ill-equipped Cypriot army. By the end of the second phase of the invasion, and despite the fact that the legitimate government of Cyprus had been restored,[1] the Turkish forces had occupied nearly 37 percent of the territory of the Republic of Cyprus, dividing the island on an east-west line. The consequences of the invasion have already been described in chapter one.

The unprecedented ferocity of the Turkish attack on Cyprus and the actions that followed removed all pretext from the justifications offered by Turkey for its actions. The ethnic cleansing that followed in the area occupied by the Turkish Army and the establishment of a puppet state in the same area[2] violated the Fourth Geneva Convention (1949) and proved that Turkey aimed at the partition of Cyprus through the creation of two states on the island. The creation of a puppet state by an occupation power has been considered illegal in twentieth-century international jurisprudence and diplomatic practice. Turkey's actions in Cyprus in 1974 and since then are in conflict with any reasonable interpretation of rights claimed by Turkey under the 1960 Treaty of Guarantee, or under any interpretation of humanitarian intervention.[3]   For example:

- During the period of the intercommunal troubles that followed the Turkish Cypriot withdrawal from the government of the Republic of Cyprus, Turkey never filed an interstate application on behalf of the Turkish Cypriots against the Republic of Cyprus alleging violations of the European Convention.
- Two days before the Greek-sponsored coup in Nicosia, the two Cypriot communities, in UN-sponsored intercommunal negotiations, had reached a new power-sharing agreement amending the problematic provisions of the 1960 Constitution.
- Turkish Cypriots had suffered no injuries during the coup against the government of Cyprus.
- Turkey had not exhausted the consultation provisions of the Treaty of Guarantee prior to its invasion of Cyprus.
- The legitimate government of Cyprus had been reestablished within days as the junta ruling Greece and the puppet regime it placed in power in Nicosia collapsed.
- Interventions under humanitarian law are limited in duration and pro- portional in scope, and do not normally affect the sovereignty, unity, or political independence of the state affected.

The use of force against a sovereign member of the UN contravened relevant provisions of the UN Charter. Any interpretation of the Treaty of Guarantee to the contrary would be in conflict with Articles 2 (para. 4) and 103 of the UN Charter.

To date, Turkey has failed to restore the status quo ante in Cyprus, which was the declared objective of the invasion. Instead, it created a puppet state in the occupied areas. Moreover, the 1983 unilateral declaration of inde- pendence by this entity violated contemporary international law, diplomatic practice, and relevant UN Security Council resolutions. It also violated the 1960 Treaty of Guarantee that prohibits the partition of Cyprus and the 1960 Constitution of Cyprus that affirms the indivisibility of the republic.[4]

Turkey, as a belligerent power, remains in control of nearly 37 percent of the territory of an independent and sovereign member of the United Na- tions and of the European Union. Under international law, Turkey is obligated to observe and apply the rules pertaining to military conflict and subsequent military occupation. This involves both combatants and the civilian population in the areas under occupation. Even in the absence of a declared war, the scale of hostilities in Cyprus during July and August 1974 constitute a case of armed conflict under Article 2 of the Fourth Geneva Convention (1949). Tur- key is one of the High Contracting Parties to that convention. Statements by the International Committee of the Red Cross, the Geneva Declaration of 30 July 1974 on Cyprus, and the Security Council resolutions adopted immediately after the commencement of the Turkish invasion make clear the belligerent nature of Turkey's actions. Thus, the UN Charter, the unanimous Security Council resolutions on Cyprus, and the Fourth Geneva Convention (1949), "Relative to the Protection of Civilian Persons in Time of War," remain the binding legal instruments for the events of July-August 1974 and since then.

Repeated UN Security Council and General Assembly resolutions on Cyprus, resolutions by regional organizations, and international court decisions:

- uphold the continuity and the legality of the Republic of Cyprus as well as its independence, sovereignty, territorial integrity, and the legitimacy of its government;
- define the illegality of Turkey's actions and the illegality of the puppet state created in occupied Cyprus by the Turkish army;
- call for the withdrawal of Turkish troops and address many of the issues related to the ethnic cleansing carried out by the Turkish army in occupied Cyprus; and
- make clear that Turkey's actions in Cyprus do not have the sanction of the Security Council, and are not part of any UN-endorsed self-defense, enforcement, or humanitarian action.

The outcome of Turkey's illegal invasion, continuing occupation, and continuing human rights violations are the focus of this and of the chapters that follow.

The European Convention and Discrimination

> The enjoyment of rights and freedoms set forth in this Convention shall be secured without discrimination on any ground such as sex, race, color, language, religion, political or other opinion, national or social origin. (Article 14, European Convention of Human Rights [1950])

> Any discrimination based on any ground such as sex, race, color, ethnic or social origin, genetic features, language, religion or belief, political or any other opinion…shall be prohibited…discrimination on grounds of nationality shall be prohibited." (Article 21, Charter of Fundamental Rights of the European Union [2000])

These two important references from the two major European human rights documents provide the foundation for the discussion that follows. The evidence presented here will show that the human rights violations committed by Turkey in the occupied areas of Cyprus in and since 1974 were directed against Greek Cypriots because of their national origin, language, and religion. Turkey ratified the European Convention of Human Rights in 1954. All the signatories of this convention are bound by its obligations. Moreover, Turkey is a prospective EU member, currently going through accession negotiations. Like all prospective EU members, Turkey is expected to comply with and implement relevant provisions of EU law in its domestic and foreign policy. The

European Convention is part of EU law. The fact that Turkey's actions in occupied Cyprus were directed against the Greek Cypriots[5] because of their national origin, language, and religion constitutes a clear violation of the European Convention. This has been affirmed by all the decisions of the European Commission of Human Rights and by the European Court of Human Rights in the four interstate applications filed by the Republic of Cyprus against Turkey.[6] The same violation has been determined in several individual cases brought by Greek Cypriots against Turkey in the European Court of Human Rights.

The admissibility decision by the European Court of Human Rights in the case of Eleni Foka[7] is the most recent statement on this subject. Foka, a Cypriot national of Greek Cypriot origin, was expelled from the occupied Karpass Peninsula in northeast Cyprus, mistreated, and prevented from returning to her home and occupation. Foka argued that the actions directed against her by the occupation authorities occurred because of her ethnic origin, religious beliefs, and opposition to Turkey's military occupation. Having examined issues of fact and law, the European Court of Human Rights declared her case admissible on 9 November 2006. Even though the Fourth Section of the European Court of Human Rights in its judgment of 24 June 2008 found in favor of the applicant in certain aspects of her case, Foka's attorneys have appealed the ruling to the plenary session of the court in order to clarify certain technical and other legal points arising from the ruling.

The European Court of Human Rights has consistently held Turkey liable for failing to secure substantive rights under the convention in areas of occupied Cyprus under its effective control. Even if Turkish Cypriot "authorities" committed some of these violations, they were also imputable to Turkey. Being in effective control, Turkey was responsible for the acts of a "subordinate local administration."[8] Turkey's continuing violations of Article 14 of the European Convention and Article 21 of the European Charter of Fundamental Rights, among other articles, present a major challenge to the European human rights regime.

Turkey, however, is not alone in its actions. The 2004 comprehensive plan for a Cyprus settlement prepared under Anglo-American auspices by former UN secretary-general Kofi Annan violated both of these conventions. It did so through derogations that violated the nondiscrimination provisions that are the foundation of the European human rights regime. For example:

- It legitimized the outcome of ethnic cleansing.
- It limited the rights of settlement and property ownership on the basis of ethnic origin.
- It was based on ethnic separation within a rigid bi-zonal bicommunal constitutional framework.
- It limited the right of refugees and the displaced to voluntarily return to their homes in peace and safety.

It is ironic that the guardian of international law was willing to advance proposals in direct violation of some of the most significant documents created for the protection and promotion of human rights. Turkey's actions in Cyprus were not unprecedented. In its recent history, Turkey had acted in a similar manner against people of non-Turkish ethnic origin living in its domain. Despite Turkish denials, the record of what occurred against Armenians, Jews, Greeks, and other minorities living in the Ottoman Empire and later in the Republic of Turkey in the first half of the twentieth century is well documented. Despite Turkey's interest in acceding to the European Union, its ratification of major European and UN human rights conventions, and the 1949 Geneva Conventions, the sad record of human rights violations continues.

The Human Dimension—Ethnic Cleansing

"Ethnic Cleansing" became part of the human rights vocabulary as a result of the events in former Yugoslavia at the end of the Cold War. These events led to the creation of the International Criminal Court by the UN Security Council and to the indictment of Serbian leaders in July 1995. A precedent had already been set for such actions by the Nuremberg and Tokyo indictments at the end of World War II.

Ethnic cleansing took place in occupied Cyprus during and after the 1974 Turkish invasion. Turkey systematically and deliberately violated the European Convention and the 1949 Fourth Geneva Convention "Relative to the Protection of Civilian Persons in Time of War."[9] This was done through a determined policy of eviction, deportation, intimidation, forced evacuation, and expulsion of Greek Cypriots living in the area that came under Turkish Army control by the middle of August 1974. As already mentioned, some 170,000 Greek Cypriots, approximately 28 percent of the island's total population, became victims of ethnic cleansing based on their ethnicity, language, and religion, in clear violation of Article 14 of the European Convention. The violations that will be described occurred during the course of military operations and since the ceasefire agreements that terminated the hostilities. These violations continue to this day. These violations are not figments of the imagination or the product of Cypriot spin masters. They have been documented by eyewitness accounts, the international media, UN reports, NGO investigations, and reports, decisions, and investigations by the European Commission of Human Rights and the European Court of Human Rights. These violations have been documented despite Turkey's noncooperation. The government of Turkey has attempted to defy its obligations under the convention by arguing that its acceptance of the convention applied only to cases within Turkey's territory. This argument has been conclusively rejected by the European Commission of Human Rights in all four applications filed by the Republic of Cyprus against Turkey, as well as by the European Court of Human Rights in the *Loizidou v. Turkey* case. Being in effective control of the occupied areas of Cyprus, Turkey was liable for the acts of its agents (that is, the Turkish military and other administrators) and those of its "subordinate local administration," namely, the "authorities" set up and supported by the Turkish army in occupied Cyprus.

The report by the European Commission of Human Rights on the first two interstate applications by Cyprus against Turkey determined by a vote of

13-1 that Turkey had violated Article 8 of the European Convention. It did so by the eviction of Greek Cypriots from their homes, by their transportation to other places within the north of Cyprus and, eventually, by their deportation across the demarcation line. The fact that these persons were not allowed to return to their homes was also a violation of the same article. Thus, the denial of the right to voluntarily return in peace and safety to one's own home was a clear indication of the deliberate act of ethnic cleansing that took place in the occupied areas of Cyprus. This act was completed by Turkey's demand that all Turkish Cypriots living in the free areas of Cyprus move north to areas under the control of the Turkish army. This was achieved by Turkey's threat of the use of force against both the Republic of Cyprus and those Turkish Cypriots who remained in the government-controlled areas.

With the determination that the occupied areas have been under Turkey's effective control since the conclusion of the hostilities in Cyprus, Turkey also violated the Fourth Geneva Convention (1949), to which it is a High Contracting Party. Specifically, Article 2 states that the convention applies to all cases of declared war or armed conflict, even if the state of war is not recognized by one of the parties. It also applies to cases of total or partial occupation of a country. Article 49 of the same explicitly prohibits individual or mass forcible population transfers, what we call today "ethnic cleansing." In addition, Article 147 of the same convention stipulates that a violation of Article 49 constitutes a grave breach of the convention requiring sanctions under Article 146 of the same. The Nuremberg indictment involving acts of Nazi officials and the mass expulsion of Poles and Alsatians became a precedent for the stipulations of the Fourth Geneva Convention.

Turkey's war acts and subsequent actions carried out by the occupation authorities and their agents in areas under their control were intended to bring about the forced exodus of legal Greek Cypriot residents of the occupied areas. These acts were directed at Greek Cypriots because of their ethnicity, language, and religion. Ethnic cleansing was achieved through acts of intimidation, indiscriminate bombing during the hostilities, killings in cold blood, separation of families, detention, terror, assault and battery, mass expulsions, and other repressive tactics that will be examined below.

The Human Dimension—Refugees and Displaced

Following the invasion of Cyprus, Turkey embarked on a deliberate policy aiming at the de facto partition of Cyprus. The 1974 two-phase invasion was the first step toward the realization of this goal. The second step was the ethnic cleansing that followed the invasion. This was necessary because of the demographic distribution of Greek and Turkish Cypriots across the island. Turkey sought to create an ethnically homogeneous region in the areas occupied by its armed forces through the expulsion of the Greek Cypriot population from their ancestral homes. Measures were also taken prohibiting their right to voluntarily return to their homes in peace and safety, despite provisions of international law and resolutions by various international organizations.

Chapter one described the economic and social costs of the dislocation created by the Turkish invasion and the gigantic efforts required of the government of the Republic of Cyprus and other organizations to provide humanitarian assistance, restore economic and social cohesion, and revive the Cypriot economy. Five years after the Turkish invasion, Cyprus was able to repair most of the structural damage of the invasion. However, the human costs and the disruption caused to Cypriot society remain. Cohesion of families and their links to ancestral lands have suffered irreparable damage.

Cyprus's successes in recovering from the effects of the invasion and occupation have enabled Turkey's supporters to excuse or justify Turkey's actions. Indeed, the humanitarian decision by the government of the Republic of Cyprus not to "palestinianize" the refugee/displaced problem has worked against it. Countries like the United States and Great Britain and certain UN mediators like former Secretary-General Kofi Annan may have found the events of and since 1974 "distasteful." However, they have not supported measures to implement unanimous Security Council resolutions, or resolutions by the UN General Assembly, the Parliamentary Assembly of the Council of Europe, or the European Parliament. These resolutions call for the voluntary return of refugees and displaced to their habitual homes and properties in peace and safety. Nor have these mediators supported sanctions against Turkey for its documented violations of human rights under various conventions. Praising Cyprus for its dramatic recovery in the aftermath of the 1974 invasion cannot hide that reality. Not many countries of the size of Cyprus could have recovered from a devastating blow such as that of the 1974 Turkish invasion. Unfortunately, that praise has been used to rationalize schemes based on the "new reality" created by the invasion and the continuing occupation. This is why discriminatory constitutional schemes have been proposed under the guise of a "bi-zonal bicommunal federation" which violate both the spirit and the letter of the European Convention and the Charter of Fundamental Rights of the European Union.

The ethnic cleansing carried out by the Turkish military and its surrogates involves two groups of Greek Cypriots, that is, the refugees and the displaced. The former are those citizens who have been expelled from, or have had to flee their habitual residence because of fear for their safety, are prevented from returning to their homes and properties, and are consequently forced to seek opportunities outside their country. This involves thousands of Greek Cypriots who sought a new life in Great Britain, Australia, and elsewhere. Internally displaced are those Cypriots who were forced from their homes and properties or were forced to flee and now live in the safety of the government-controlled areas. They did so in order to avoid the effects of armed conflict, violations of their rights under the European Convention, and threats to their lives. These persons have not crossed an internationally recognized state border as in the case of refugees.[10] These terms are often used interchangeably.

The reality of the magnitude of the problem of the displaced and the refugees has been amply documented in the reports of the European Commission of Human Rights and the European Court of Human Rights in the four interstate applications filed by Cyprus against Turkey. In the report on the first two cases, the European Commission of Human Rights made it clear that the massive population movement from the northern to the southern part of Cyprus in the aftermath of the invasion was a matter of public knowledge and an indisputable fact. Therefore, the commission required no further investigation, especially in view of the documentation available from other international organizations and, in particular, the United Nations. Thus, on the displacement of persons, the European Commission of Human Rights determined by a vote of 13-1[11] that, by its continued refusal to allow the return of more than 170,000 Greek Cypriot refugees and displaced to their habitual homes and properties, Turkey violated and continued to violate Article 8 (respect for private and family life and for the home) of the convention. The commission also determined that Turkey exercised de facto jurisdiction in areas under its control. By a vote of 12-1, the European Commission of Human Rights ruled that the eviction of Greek Cypriots from their homes, their transportation to other places within northern Cyprus, and their eventual deportation across the cease-fire line was another violation of Article 8 of the convention. Similarly, by a vote of 14-1, the commission found that the separation of Greek Cypriot families brought about by the displacement of people constituted yet another violation of Article 8 of the European Convention. By similar votes, Turkey was also found guilty of continuing violations of Article 8 of the European Convention in the case of the displacement of persons and the separation of families in the third Cypriot interstate application against Turkey.

The European Court of Human Rights issued its judgment on the fourth Cypriot interstate application on 10 May 2001.[12] This is a historic case in which the court pronounced on the overall legal consequences of Turkey's invasion and continuing occupation of Cyprus. The judgment, in no uncertain terms, reaffirmed that the government of the Republic of Cyprus is the sole legitimate government of Cyprus. It determined that the so-called "TRNC" is not a state under international law; that it is illegal, and survives by virtue of Turkish military support. Being in effective control over northern Cyprus, Turkey is responsible for securing all human rights under the convention and its protocols. Turkey has ratified these legal instruments. Consequently, all human rights violations are imputable to it. Turkey was also held responsible for the acts of private individuals if it acquiesced or connived in acts that violated the convention.

In the case of the Greek Cypriot displaced/refugees, this important decision upheld their right to return to their homes and properties. Actions denying this right violate Article 1, Protocol I of the convention. The denial of this right could not be justified because of a potential settlement of the overall crisis that may be reached by ongoing intercommunal talks, or by the need to house displaced Turkish Cypriots.[13]

In addition to the conclusions of the European Commission of Human Rights and of the European Court of Human Rights in the four Cypriot interstate applications, there are decisions on individual cases adjudicated by the European Court of Human Rights involving the properties of displaced Greek Cypriots. The property issue will be examined in detail later in this volume.

The right of the refugees and the displaced to voluntarily return in peace and safety to their ancestral and habitual homes has also been recognized and upheld by numerous resolutions adopted by the United Nations Security Council,[14] the UN General Assembly,[15] the Parliamentary Assembly of the Council of Europe, the legislative organ of the Council of Europe,[16] and the European Parliament, the legislative instrument of the European Union.[17] The condemnation of ethnic cleansing in recent years has not been isolated to the Cyprus case. Even more explicit denunciations of this practice can be found in UN General Assembly Resolution 42/121 of 18 December 1992, describing the practice of ethnic cleansing akin to genocide, and in resolutions adopted by the UN Security Council in 1993 in the case of Bosnia. The practice of ethnic cleansing, according to these resolutions, is unlawful and unacceptable. In the Bosnian case, the Security Council has asked, unequivocally, for the reversal of the consequences of ethnic cleansing and upheld the right of all refugees to return to their homes. Unfortunately, for reasons already discussed, in the case of Cyprus the UN Security Council has yet to implement this philosophy into practical measures.

An interesting subsidiary issue arising from the fate of Cypriot refugees is evident in the resolution adopted on 13 June 1985 by the European Parliament on behalf of a Cypriot refugee couple, Katerina and Vassilis Nicola. They lost their home in occupied Cyprus and could not return there. These persons were faced with a deportation order by British immigration authorities. The European Parliament's resolution called for granting to them refugee status with indefinite stay in the United Kingdom. The resolution also asked that similar deportations of Cypriot refugees be stopped. This is not the place to discuss British immigration policy. It is, however, one more example of the plight facing refugees as a result of the Turkish invasion. The UN Commission on Human Rights[18] has also adopted resolutions on behalf of the Greek Cypriot displaced/refugees.

Repeatedly, objective international third parties have documented the plight and the seriousness of the problems confronting Greek Cypriot displaced and refugees. Resolutions and decisions of international organizations remain unimplemented for reasons discussed in chapter three of this volume. The author's position remains that failure to live up to the requirements of European and international law undermines the European human rights regime and the European commitment to democracy, the rule of law, and human rights. No viable solution can come about unless the right of the refugees and the displaced to voluntarily return in peace and safety to their ancestral and habitual homes becomes part of any future solution and the consequences of ethnic cleansing are reversed.

The Human Dimension—Ethnic Cleansing Techniques

In addition to forced expulsions of Greek Cypriots from occupied Cyprus, the Turkish Army and the occupation authorities employed a variety of other techniques to implement their policy of ethnic cleansing. These documented and gross violations of human rights will be examined in this section. Most of these violations occurred during and immediately after the cessation of hostilities until the ethnic cleansing was completed. However, some of these violations have continued, especially in the case of the enclaved Greek Cypriots. The issue of the enclaved will be examined further in chapter five. In its ruling of 10 May 2001 in the fourth Cypriot interstate application against Turkey, the European Court of Human Rights concluded that the problems of the enclaved, refugees, and displaced were compounded by the absence of effective domestic remedies, which was a direct violation of Article 13 of the European Convention[19]. In the case of the displaced/refugees, access to effective remedies in the occupied areas was affected by the prohibition on the movement of Greek Cypriots across the ceasefire line. This practice lasted until 13 April 2003, when the occupation forces eased crossing restrictions without eliminating any of the consequences of ethnic cleansing or remedying any of the human rights violations.

Separation of Families

This has been one of the direct consequences of the Turkish invasion and of the ethnic cleansing of the occupied areas. Separation of families is of particular significance not only for humanitarian reasons, but also because of the social structure of Cypriot society. Separation of families occurred during and in the aftermath of the hostilities in areas of northern Cyprus that came under Turkish Army control. Greek Cypriots fled to protect their lives and avoid the systematic terror carried out by the occupation forces. Those Greek Cypriots who were unable to leave or decided to stay in their homes faced deportation, expulsion, false detention, intimidation, inhuman treatment, and transportation to other areas of northern Cyprus prior to their expulsion. These actions were directed against these Greek Cypriots because of their ethnic origin, language, and religion. The Red Cross, government social agencies, and other volunteer organizations struggled to identify and reunite families, in some cases months after the invasion and the ethnic cleansing of occupied Cyprus. This was a clear violation of Article 8 (respect for the family and home) of the European Convention. It was one of the violations brought to the attention of the European Commission of Human Rights and later to the European Court of Human Rights by the four interstate applications filed against Turkey by the Republic of Cyprus.

In the report on the first two interstate applications covering the period of 20 July 1974 to 18 May 1976, the European Commission of Human Rights by a vote of 14-1 determined that, by its policies and actions, Turkey had violated Article 8 (respect for the family and the home). The third (1977) interstate application by Cyprus against Turkey covered events since 18 May 1976, when the European Commission terminated its investigation of the first two Cypriot interstate applications. Again, by a vote of 14-1, the commission determined that the continued separation of families resulting from Turkey's refusal to allow the return of Greek Cypriots to their family members in the north was a continuing violation of Article 8 of the European Convention. Similar were the conclusions of the European Court of Human Rights in the historic decision on the fourth Cypriot interstate application against Turkey (10

May 2001). By a vote of 16-1, the court determined that there had been a continuing violation of Article 8 of the convention by reason of the refusal to allow Greek Cypriot displaced persons to return to their homes in northern Cyprus and the absence of effective remedies under Article 13 of the convention. Turkey's continuing actions also violated Articles 25 and 27 of the Fourth Geneva Convention. Thus, both the European Commission of Human Rights and the European Court of Human Rights have documented by overwhelming votes the continuing disrespect and violation of private and family life in the case of the Greek Cypriot displaced and the refugees. In the absence of sanctions, these violations continue.

Respect for the Home, Home Life, and Deprivation of Possessions

An additional consequence of ethnic cleansing has been the issue of the respect for the home and home life and the deprivation, looting, and wanton destruction of possessions. This closely relates to the separation of families discussed above. In all its four interstate applications, the government of Cyprus pointed to violations of Article 8 (par. 1) of the European Convention and of Article 1, Protocol I of the same convention. Article 8 addressed specifically the right of respect for the private life and home, while Article 1 of Protocol I spoke specifically of the right to the peaceful enjoyment of possessions and not being deprived of personal possessions. Both the European Commission of Human Rights and the European Court of Human Rights, by overwhelming majorities, found Turkey in violation of both articles. The historic European Court decision on the fourth Cypriot interstate application (10 May 2001) affirms in no uncertain terms by a vote of 16-1 the continuing violation of Article 8 of the convention because of the refusal to allow any of the Greek Cypriot displaced to return to their homes in occupied Cyprus. By the same vote, Turkey was also found guilty of violating Article 1, Protocol I of the convention because Greek Cypriots were denied access to, control over, and enjoyment of their properties, as well as any compensation for the interference with their property rights. Turkey was also in violation of Article 13 because of the absence of effective remedies for those not residing in the occupied areas. It is important to note that the decision on the fourth interstate application addressed clearly the "continuing" nature of these violations, which have gone on long after the Turkish invasion and its aftermath.

The issue of the respect of the home and of the systematic deprivation of possessions, looting, pillage, and wanton property destruction arose in the occupied areas during and in the aftermath of the Turkish invasion. This was a violation of Articles 33 and 53 of the Fourth Geneva Convention. Greek Cypriots were systematically forced out of their homes and fled for their lives during and in the aftermath of the invasion. Their personal property, including their homes, were seized, and movable property was removed by Turkish soldiers. Media reports showed looted property, including cars, buses, household goods, etc., in cities in southern Turkey. Turkish naval vessels transported these possessions to the Turkish mainland. Greek Cypriot homes and furnishings were distributed to Turkish Cypriots and later on to illegal Turkish settlers. Similar was the fate of agricultural goods, industrial goods, and tourist facilities that fell into the hands of the invading forces. Wanton destruction of property was also a tactic used to support ethnic cleansing. Buildings along the ceasefire line were burned along with orchards and crops belonging to Greek Cypriots. Religious and archaeological properties bore the brunt of this wanton destruction and looting. This issue and the issue of property will be examined more fully below.

The lack of respect for the home and home life, and the deprivation of possessions, looting, and wanton destruction of property that took place during and after the invasion had one objective, namely, to ethnically cleanse the occupied areas from its Greek Cypriot inhabitants because of their ethnicity, religion, and language. These violations have yet to be remedied.

The reader should also note that, as in previous investigations, Turkey, as the respondent state, failed to cooperate as required with the investigations of the instruments of the Council of Europe. Moreover, the lone vote cast against the findings of the European Court of Human Rights and the European Commission of Human Rights was that of the Turkish representative.

Robbery, Looting, and Wanton Destruction

The destruction of property is closely connected with violations identified in the preceding section of this chapter. Article 33 of the Fourth Geneva Convention prohibits pillage and reprisals against persons and property, while Article 53 prohibits the destruction of real or personal property, whether publicly or privately owned, unless the destruction was the direct result of military operations. In turn, Article 1 of Protocol I of the European Convention declares that "every natural or legal person is entitled to the peaceful enjoyment of his possessions" and that "no one shall be deprived of his possessions."

The Cypriot complaints in this area were part of the first two Cypriot interstate applications against Turkey. By votes of 12-1 the European Commission of Human Rights determined that Greek Cypriots had been deprived, on a large scale, of their possessions. This deprivation was not an act carried out in the public interest. Persons committing these acts were acting under the direct order or authority of the Turkish forces. This is why these actions were imputed to Turkey under the convention. The charges included eviction, seizure of movable property, and its removal by Turkish Army vehicles or requisitioned vehicles. In addition to movable property, the widespread looting included agricultural crops, manufactured goods, vehicles, farm animals, household goods, building equipment, and so on. What could not be carried away was often destroyed. That included homes, religious property, farm animals, and religious and archaeological sites. Again, the objective of these actions was clear: to create fear, to force the Greek Cypriots to leave for the safety of the government-controlled areas, and to eradicate the Greek Cypriot cultural heritage in the occupied areas. As in the case of the other violations identified in this chapter, there were no effective remedies as required by the convention for the injuries suffered.

Rape and Forced Prostitution

Article 3 of the European Convention provides that "no one shall be subjected to torture or to inhuman or degrading treatment." Article 27 of the Fourth Geneva Convention specifically calls for the protection of women against attacks on their honor, especially rape, enforced prostitution, or other indecent assault. The Turkish Army violated both conventions in its attempt to intimidate and humiliate the Greek Cypriot population and to create conditions of fear in order to force them to leave their homes for the safety of the government-controlled areas. These brutal acts were directed at Greek Cypriot women and children because of their ethnicity, religion, and language. The humiliation and dishonoring of women and children was an even more serious offense because of the traditional nature of Cypriot society, which values highly family honor and the honor of female family members and children.

In its report on the first two Cypriot interstate applications, the European Commission of Human Rights examined the allegations of rape and forced prostitution.[20] The same was done by the investigation of the German NGO Asme-Humanitas in its report of 19 July 1977.[21] Both conclude that the available evidence documents the charges included in the Cypriot interstate applications and find Turkey guilty of violating Article 3 of the convention. By a vote of 12-1, the European Commission of Human Rights found that the incidents of rape constituted "inhuman treatment" under Article 3 of the European Convention that is imputable to Turkey. Evidence was obtained from witnesses, including Turkish military personnel, medical doctors, and victims. The evidence shows repeated rapes of women and children from the ages of twelve to seventy-one to such an extent that the victims suffered major physical and/or psychological damage. Evidence was also presented where women of a particular village were collected and placed in separate rooms of empty houses to be raped repeatedly by Turkish soldiers, including officers. Some rapes took place in the presence of family members and other children. The victims included pregnant and retarded persons. Some of the captors and abusers killed their victims. The European Commission of Human Rights concluded that these rapes were not isolated cases of indiscipline. No evidence was presented that the Turkish authorities took measures to prevent this from happening, or that any disciplinary action was taken following such incidents.

This was one more tactic involved in the ethnic cleansing of the occupied areas. It created conditions of fear and intimidation that forced Greek Cypriots to leave their homes. The Fourth Geneva Convention (Article 147) finds these actions to be a grave violation of the convention requiring international penalties. None have been levied against Turkey.

Torture, Inhuman Treatment, Assault and Battery, and Murder

Turkish forces and their surrogates carried out these actions that violated the European Convention and the Fourth Geneva Convention. There is no evidence of measures taken by the Turkish authorities to prevent such occurrences or to penalize those responsible for them. These actions were directed at Greek Cypriots because of their ethnicity, religion, and language. Once again, the objective of these actions was intimidation leading to the ethnic cleansing of the occupied areas.

Article 3 of the Fourth Geneva Convention is explicit in addressing the prohibition of cruel, degrading, and humiliating treatment or torture. Reference has already been made to Article 27 of the same convention in the case of the treatment of women, rape, and indecent assault. Even more explicit is Article 147 that prohibits willful killing, torture, and inhuman treatment, including biological experiments.[22] This article finds these actions to be a grave violation of the convention. Those committing such violations are liable to sanctions. For reasons already stated, Turkey's allies have shielded Turkey from any sanctions despite the available documented evidence. The European Commission of Human Rights and the Asme-Humanitas report on Cyprus documented cases of assault and battery, as well as murder and killing of noncombatant civilians regardless of sex and age, as well as military personnel and POWs. Even more damning is the evidence presented before the European Commission of Human Rights and the commission's conclusions in the first two interstate applications filed by the Republic of Cyprus against Turkey in 1974 and 1975.

The European Commission of Human Rights found Turkey in violation of Article 2 of the European Convention. The said article states that "everyone's right to life shall be protected by law. No one shall be deprived of his life intentionally." By an overwhelming vote of 14-1, the only negative vote being that of the Turkish representative, the commission found evidence that indicated that killings were committed on a "substantial scale" and that such deprivation of life was not justified. The commission documented the killing of Greek Cypriots in bombing raids on civilian targets, including hospitals, by the use of napalm. The commission found these actions to be breaches of the Fourth Geneva Convention, rather than of the European Convention. The Turkish Army and its surrogates embarked on a systematic course of murder of civilians unconnected with any war activity, including women, children, and POWs. As in other instances, Turkey failed to cooperate in the commission's investigation.

The issue of inhuman treatment is prohibited under the European Convention. Such treatment was documented by the testimony of hundreds of civilians, including the elderly, women, and children. The evidence indicated that civilians were victims of systematic torture and humiliating treatment while in Turkish detention. These tactics were intended to spread fear and intimidation to Greek Cypriots so that they would be forced to leave for the safety of the government-controlled areas. These witnesses provided evidence of severe beatings, whipping, beating with electric clubs, extinction of cigarettes on their skin, piercing them with bayonets, and so on. Many of those who were mistreated suffered mental and physical wounds. Hundreds of civilians transported and imprisoned in Turkey reported similar treatment. Much of this mistreatment occurred after the end of hostilities in a deliberate attempt to terrorize the Greek Cypriot population of the occupied areas.

The European Commission of Human Rights by a vote of 12-1 confirmed the ill-treatment of persons in captivity. In a similar vote, the withholding of adequate food, water, and medical treatment to Greek Cypriot detainees in Cyprus and Turkey was also a violation of Article 3 of the convention. The same was true of the mistreatment of Greek Cypriots not in detention.

Before closing this section, it should be mentioned that the killings of civilians in cold blood continued even after the ethnic cleansing of the occupied areas was completed. In August 1996, peaceful demonstrations for the reunification of Cyprus took place in the free areas of Cyprus along the demarcation line. Two young Greek Cypriots were murdered in cold blood and several were wounded, including two members of the UN peacekeeping force, when security forces and members of the Turkish terrorist group "Grey Wolves" opened fire against unarmed Greek Cypriot demonstrators. The investigation that followed showed the official involvement and participation of the Turkish forces, Turkish Cypriot officials, and a large contingent of the "Grey Wolves." This Turkish group had been brought into occupied Cyprus by the Turkish authorities. The killings and the participation of the occupation authorities were denounced in a sharply worded resolution adopted by the European Parliament on 19 September 1996. The resolution called on Turkey to take "all necessary measures" to identify, arrest, and bring to justice all those implicated in the murders and in the decision to fire on unarmed civilians. Turkey and its subordinate local administration in occupied Cyprus have yet to comply with this resolution. Another similar incident took place a few weeks later, when an unarmed Greek Cypriot was murdered near the village of Achna in the vicinity of the British base at Dhekelia. In a resolution adopted on 24 October 1996, the European Parliament again expressed its shock over the latest "cold blooded murder" of a Greek Cypriot by the "Turkish occupation army." It asked the European Union's Commission and the EU Council of Ministers to "inform the Turkish occupation forces" of the "deep indignation" of the EU in regard to this incident. The resolution in other operative paragraphs spoke of Turkey's continuing violations of human rights in Cyprus and concluded that Turkey's future relations with the EU depended partially on Turkey's policy on Cyprus.[23] This was an important linkage of Turkey's human rights obligations and its EU aspirations.

On 23 December 1996, the UN Security Council unanimously adopted Resolution 1092. In addition to extending the mandate of the UN peacekeeping force in Cyprus, the Security Council deplored these violent incidents and the disproportionate use of force by the "Turkish/Turkish Cypriot side." Under Anglo-American pressure this resolution attempted to temper its criticism of Turkey's actions by calling for measures not to disturb conditions along the buffer zone and for the Cypriot police to be more active in controlling Greek Cypriot demonstrations. This was one more indication of the political realities facing the Cyprus problem and the protection of human rights in Cyprus.

The families of those killed in cold blood during these incidents brought cases against Turkey in the European Court of Human Rights. On 24 June 2008, the court issued separate judgments in the cases of *Solomou and Others v. Turkey*, Application No. 36832/97, and *Isaak v. Turkey*, Application No. 44587/98. In both judgments, Turkey was found guilty of violating Articles 1 and 2 of the European Convention. The court awarded financial damages to the families of those killed. In addition, it concluded that:

- there were no effective remedies available to those affected by the killings;
- there was no effective investigation by the occupation authorities;
- there was disproportionate use of lethal force by the security forces;
- the killings took place with the tacit agreement of agents of Turkey;
- more than eleven years after the incidents, notwithstanding available photographic evidence, none of those responsible for the killings had been identified or arraigned; and
- Turkey was responsible for acts violating the convention outside its territory because it was in effective control of areas of Cyprus under its occupation.

Deprivation of Liberty and False Detention

Actions by the Turkish forces during and after the invasion raised additional questions about Turkey's human rights violations, particularly of Article 5 of the European Convention. This article guarantees the right to liberty and the security of the person by public authorities. The Turkish actions violated Article 49 of the Geneva Convention that prohibits individual or mass transfers of persons from an occupied territory to the territory of the occupying power, regardless of motives. In addition, Articles 42-45 and 79-135 provide specifically for conditions of detention, etc. The violations of both the European Convention and the Fourth Geneva Convention have also been confirmed by the investigative report of Asme-Humanitas.

The European Commission of Human Rights investigated violations of Article 5 of the European Convention that were raised in the first two Cypriot interstate applications against Turkey. The Cypriot complaints charged that the Turkish forces arbitrarily detained thousands of persons. The persons routinely rounded up included women and children. Men were separated from their families, while women, children, and the elderly were placed in "concentration camps" or were expelled. They were kept in crowded, unsanitary conditions at the height of summertime, when temperatures reach 100° F and above. The worst cases were the camps at Voni, Marathovouno, Vitsada, and Gypsou. Many civilian males between seventeen and seventy years of age were sent to camps on the outskirts of occupied Nicosia, while others were transported to Turkey and detained in prisons in Adana, Amasia, and other locations in violation of the Fourth Geneva Convention. Turkey never provided complete lists of detainees as required by international law. Some three thousand persons were still unaccounted for in 1976, when Cyprus filed its first interstate application against Turkey. The issue of the missing will be examined in the next chapter.

As in the rest of the allegations against it, Turkey refused to cooperate with the investigation of the European Commission of Human Rights. The commission determined by a vote of 13-1 that the confinement of thousands of Greek Cypriots in detention centers violated Article 5 of the convention. By similar votes the commission determined that the detention of Greek Cypriot civilian and military personnel in Turkey violated the same convention article.

In Conclusion

Looking back at the evidence presented in this chapter, a number of conclusions are warranted:

- Independent investigations of the allegations made by the Republic of Cyprus in its interstate applications against Turkey prove beyond doubt Turkey's culpability for violations of international law and specific treaties that Turkey ratified and pledged to uphold.
- The overwhelming votes of the European Commission of Human Rights and the European Court of Human Rights, Turkey's noncooperation with the instruments of the Council of Europe, and the one negative vote consistently cast by the Turkish member of the commission and the court show Turkey's determined and intentional violation of international law and of Turkey's international obligations.
- These investigations have also shown the absence of effective remedies for the victims of these violations.
- These investigations have also shown that the Turkish authorities have taken no measures or imposed no penalties for the misconduct of anyone acting under the control or authority of the occupation forces. As shown, Turkey is responsible for the conduct of its agents and of its surrogates in occupied Cyprus.
- The violations analyzed in this chapter were deliberate and were directed against Greek Cypriots because of their ethnicity, religion, and language.
- The objective of these deliberate actions was to intimidate and create terror and fear among innocent Greek Cypriot civilians. They fled their homes seeking safety in the government-controlled area of Cyprus. These tactics, along with the forcible expulsion of thousands of Greek Cypriots, helped Turkey achieve its goal of ethnic cleansing.

The sad record of the documented violations of human rights by Turkey in Cyprus raises the issue of the effectiveness of the European human rights regime. As shown in chapter three, while the judicial and quasi-judicial organs of the Council of Europe have performed as designed, the implementation of their decisions remains entangled in political and security considerations. This is a serious problem when dealing with a country like Turkey, whose diplomacy has rallied the support of key international players that have helped it avoid sanctions for its international misconduct.

CHAPTER FIVE

Invasion, Occupation, and Ethnic Cleansing:
The Human Dimension

THE EFFECTS of the Turkish invasion were felt throughout Cyprus. However, the fate of three special Greek Cypriot groups deserves special attention. These groups include the missing, the enclaved, and refugees and displaced persons. Chapter four addressed broad issues affecting the displaced and refugees. Property issues affecting this group will be discussed in the next chapter.

The Missing

The issue of the missing remains one of the most tragic ongoing consequences of the 1974 Turkish invasion. A total of 1,619 Greek Cypriots were listed as missing since 1974. This number is now declining as the Committee on Missing Persons (CMP) continues the identification of remains found in various areas of occupied Cyprus. The number of missing is significant, particularly if taken in proportion to the 1974 population of Cyprus.[1] Even though there have been other cases of disappearances involving opponents of authoritarian regimes, as in Argentina, the case of the Greek Cypriot missing is different. It is the direct outcome of the Turkish invasion. In contrast to traditional notions of MIAs, that is, military personnel missing as a result of protracted hostilities, 39 percent of the Greek Cypriot missing are civilians captured by the Turkish forces during military operations between 20 July and 16 August 1974 in the northern part of Cyprus.

In my numerous trips to Cyprus, I have personally experienced the continuing tragedy of the families of the missing. I have had discussions and individual meetings with many families of missing persons. I have observed the vigils held by women of all ages, relatives and spouses of the missing, at crossing points into the occupied areas of Cyprus. Dressed in black and carrying photos of their missing kin, these women, for more than thirty years, have been waiting for news on their loved ones, a moving testimonial to this tragedy.

The Greek Cypriots call these persons "agnooumenoi," persons whose fate is not known. Amnesty International speaks of "disappearances." Most official documents speak of "missing persons." The Greek term holds out hope for the return of these missing persons.

Even with the recent identification through DNA techniques of some of the remains that have been exhumed, most families of the missing have not given up hope in their search for those who may still be alive somewhere in Turkey. The reader unfamiliar with Cyprus should be aware of the closely knit nature of Cypriot society in general and family in particular. There is a deeply felt need to bring closure to the loss of a family member through recovery and burial that conforms to customs and traditions that have been followed for thousands of years.[2] This is why many foreign diplomats cannot understand the emotion evoked by the issue of the missing in Cyprus and often complain that a primarily humanitarian issue has taken political dimensions. While sensitivity is needed to avoid causing unnecessary distress to the relatives of the missing, the passage of time and the lack of accounting have deepened the wounds of these families. According to the decision of the European Court of Human Rights on the fourth Cypriot interstate application against Turkey (10 May 2001), this amounts to cruel and unusual punishment.

The following data on the Greek Cypriot missing tell the story:[3] Of the 1,619 missing Greek Cypriots, 992, or 61 percent, were military personnel, reservists, or active duty. The other 511 persons, or 39 percent, were civilians, of whom 116 were females. In terms of age distribution, the figures are also telling:

Aged Over 60:	men 257	women 58
Aged 40-60:	men 226	women 15
Aged 16-39:	men 995	women 41
Under 16:	males 25	females 2

Included in this group were 8 U.S. citizens of Cypriot origin who happened to be in Cyprus during the Turkish invasion. The death of one of them was verified after the U.S. Congress repeatedly demanded that Turkey account for the fate of the missing U.S. nationals.[4] The missing persons were detained by Turkish military or by Turkish Cypriot irregular forces under Turkish military command. Many were transported to Turkey and kept in Turkish jails. They were never repatriated when the exchange of prisoners and detainees took place. Eye witness accounts, records by the International Committee of the Red Cross, photos circulated in the media, and interviews broadcast on Turkish radio place these persons in Turkish custody. When last seen, these persons were alive. Turkey refuses to account for their fate and has never produced its own record of names of Cypriot detainees as required by the Geneva Convention. In 1975, Amnesty International submitted to the Turkish government a list of forty missing persons, seeking information as to their fate. There has yet to be any response from the Turkish government to this request, or to any other calls for information by the European Commission of Human Rights, the European Court of Human Rights, or UN-related agencies.

Turkey's silence on the matter of the missing is an indirect acknowledgement of its complicity in this humanitarian drama. On 3 January 1996, Turkish Cypriot leader Rauf Denktash, who, at the time, claimed the title of "president" of the unrecognized "TRNC," gave an interview to the Turkish Cypriot press and to the Greek Cypriot TV channel Sigma. In it, he admitted that the Turkish Army turned over to Turkish Cypriot forces many of these captives, who were executed by them. The killing of innocent civilian and military captives is a violation not only of the Third and Fourth Geneva Conventions (1949) but also of several articles of the European Convention that will be examined in this chapter. These crimes are imputable to Turkey, as all international institutions agree that Turkey was and is in effective control of occupied Cyprus and therefore liable for acts of commission or omission by its agents or those of its surrogates. The issue of the missing and their fate is one more proof that Turkey's invasion of Cyprus was anything but a "peace operation," as Turkey has repeatedly claimed. The issue of the missing points to the fact that Turkey's actions and those of its surrogates were directed against Greek Cypriots because of their ethnicity, language, and religion. This was a clear case of discrimination under Article 14 of the European Convention.

The Search for the Missing

On 9 December 1975, some sixteen months after the Turkish invasion of Cyprus, the UN General Assembly adopted Resolution 3450(XXX) on the issue of the missing in Cyprus. The resolution requested the secretary-general, in cooperation with the International Committee of the Red Cross (ICRC), to "assist in the tracing and accounting for missing persons as a result of armed conflict in Cyprus." It also called on the secretary-general to provide the UN Commission on Human Rights with relevant information on the implementation of this resolution.

After protracted negotiations, more than five years later, on 22 April 1981, the UN special representative on Cyprus, Hugo J. Gobbi, announced the establishment of a Committee on Missing Persons in Cyprus (CMP). The announcement included the committee's terms of reference.[5] The three members of the committee included one "humanitarian person" each from the Greek and Turkish Cypriot communities, while the secretary-general would appoint the third person. Notable was the absence of Turkey. This was part of Turkey's systematic policy of evading responsibility for what has happened in Cyprus during and since the invasion, and of the attempt to elevate the status of the Turkish Cypriot surrogate leaders. In addition, this tripartite committee was one more deliberate step on the part of Turkey to redefine the discussion of the Cyprus problem from one of invasion, occupation, and continuing violation of human rights to a mere intercommunal dispute. In this manner, Turkey could again argue that the issue of the missing was a case of communal incompatibility, which could be remedied by ethnic separation and by the creation of two ethnically cleansed states on Cyprus.

Turkey also argued that there were no missing Greek Cypriots other than those killed during the coup in Cyprus and the Turkish "peace operation." Turkey also tried to redefine the issue of the missing by calling for an investigation of the cases of Turkish Cypriot missing from the period of the intercommunal troubles in the mid-1960s, instead of focusing on the consequences of its 1974 invasion of Cyprus. For these reasons it took the CMP three more years after its establishment to agree on procedural rules regarding its meetings, relations with the press and media, relations with the families of the missing, the number of cases to be examined, and principles guiding its investigations. This agreement was finally reached on 14 March 1984.

The CMP's terms of reference provided that the meetings would be under the direction of representatives of the communities on a rotating and monthly basis. Committee decisions would be taken by consensus, with the UN-appointed third member having the burden of assisting the committee to reach a consensus. The proceedings were "strictly confidential." Paragraph 11 was the critical paragraph of the agreement. It stated: "the Committee will not attempt to attribute responsibility for the deaths of any missing persons or make findings as to the cause of such deaths." This, clearly, limited the mandate of the committee and, as will be shown in the next section of this chapter, became a major issue in the ruling of the European Court of Human Rights in the fourth Cypriot interstate application (10 May 2001). Any disinterment was to be handled by the ICRC under its customary procedures, while the committee was to draw "comprehensive lists of missing persons of both communities, specifying as appropriate whether they are alive or dead, and in the latter case the approximate time of death." It took ten more years after the committee agreed on its procedures to bring about another agreement on "Guidelines for Investigations." This was achieved on 21 September 1994.

The CMP's work was stymied until well into the year 2005. A number of factors account for the committee's relative ineffectiveness, including:

- Turkey's noncooperation that was also reflected in the obstructionist tactics of the Turkish Cypriot member of the CMP;
- the ineffectiveness of the UN-appointed representative;
- budgetary problems that affected the CMP's access to quality technical support for its work;
- the limited scope of the CMP's mandate and the requirement for consensus-based decisions. The CMP was and still is not empowered to carry out investigations in Turkey or to investigate actions of Turkish officials and military personnel on Cypriot territory;
- the mistrust among CMP members;
- the reluctance of witnesses to testify, their fading memory of events, the death of witnesses, and the inability of the CMP to compel witnesses to testify;[6] and
- heavy construction work and land use projects that placed burial sites at risk.

The CMP's working conditions and effectiveness improved after 2005. This positive change is largely due to:

- the more cooperative attitude of the newly appointed Turkish Cypriot member. This can be attributed largely to new instructions from Ankara because of strong warnings from the EU and the Council of Europe, and the decision of the European Court of Human Rights in the fourth Cypriot interstate application (10 May 2001). This decision also addressed the issue of the missing and Turkey's responsibility in this matter. The timing was critical, as in the fall of 2005 Turkey started accession negotiations with the EU. These talks had an important influence in moderating Turkey's intransigence;

- better technical assistance by the Argentine Forensic Anthropology Team (EAAF), which operated out of new laboratories in the old Nicosia International Airport. The EAAF replaced the British "Inforce Foundation." Agreement on the new laboratories was reached on 29 September 2005;
- additional funding for the CMP's technical work made available by the government of the Republic of Cyprus and other EU members; and
- the appointment on 7 March 2006 of Christophe Girod as the third member of the CMP to replace Pierre Guberan.

Increasing progress has been made since 2005. The EAAF has located, exhumed, and identified via DNA a number of missing persons. Approximately 270 remains have undergone forensic identification, as a result of which 85 of the 1,619 Greek Cypriot missing have now been identified.[7] The focus on exhumations and DNA identification of victims has not closed the issue of the search for those who may still be alive. Turkey's lack of cooperation has been the main obstacle. The CMP's work is reaching a critical stage as the identification of the remains of the missing is beginning to bring closure to some of the families. They will now need psychological support for their loss. This phase, unfortunately, confirms the worst-case scenario for many of these families, who will never know the cause of death or the party responsible for the loss of their loved ones.

In one recent case, the family of one missing person whose remains were exhumed and identified in July 2007 has now filed a case with the European Court of Human Rights. Forensic examination of the remains showed that Demetris Koutras Charalambous was tortured and shot twice in the head. The deceased was forty-seven years old at the time of his arrest on 15 August 1974. He was last seen alive on that date by his family in the village of Eptakomi in occupied Cyprus. The case filed against Turkey points to the fact that the Turkish forces and/or their surrogates unlawfully and illegally arrested the victim, deprived him of his liberty and, eventually, of his life.

Another recent case of the continuing drama of the missing is the evidence that an injured Greek Cypriot by the name of Christakis Georgiou was alive when he was transported to Turkey in the aftermath of the invasion. Turkey has not accounted for his fate, and now the CMP has been given all relevant evidence in the hope that Turkey will cooperate in ascertaining his fate. These are examples of the challenges facing the CMP in tracing the missing because of the committee's limited mandate and Turkey's noncooperation.

International Law and the Missing

The issue of the missing brings us back to the theme underlying this discussion, that of violations of the European Convention. Turkey is a High Contracting Party to that convention. All of Turkey's actions were directed against Greek Cypriots because of their ethnicity, language, and religion. In addition to violations of Article 14 of the convention (discrimination), the issue of the missing involves numerous violations of Article 2 (right to life), Article 3 (no torture or inhuman treatment), Article 5 (right to liberty and security of the person), and Article 8 (respect for private and family life and home).

The issue of the missing also involves major infractions of the 1949 Geneva Conventions, both the third (on POW's) and the fourth (civilians). These major violations have been documented and addressed by the Council of Europe, the United Nations, the European Parliament, and the UN Commission on Human Rights. Despite recent progress, the issue of the missing remains largely unresolved, as issues of responsibility, the cause of death, and investigations in Turkey are beyond the scope of the CMP's terms of reference. Even though the problem of the missing has been approached primarily as a humanitarian issue, it has been, from the start, highly political and contentious. Turkey's noncooperation and disregard of international decisions on the missing has made this a politically charged issue. This is evident also in the justified struggle of the families of the missing to bring closure to this issue after more than three decades.

Throughout this study we have discussed the significance of actions taken by the European Commission of Human Rights and the European Court of Human Rights on Cyprus. How did these institutions respond to the issue of the missing? In the report on the first two interstate applications by Cyprus against Turkey adopted on 10 July 1976 and declassified on 31 August 1979, the European Commission of Human Rights noted the problem created by its lack of access to Turkish officials and military and detention sites. On the basis of available evidence, the commission acknowledged that it was widely accepted that a "considerable number" of Greek Cypriots were missing as a result of the conflict between Cyprus and Turkey, and that a number of the missing had been identified as being prisoners of the Turkish Army. This is why (paragraph 351) the report of the European Commission of Human Rights concluded that there was a "presumption of responsibility" by Turkey for the fate of persons in its custody. However, due to lack of access, the commission was unable to determine if the missing had been deprived of life.

The European Commission of Human Rights report on the third Cypriot interstate application was adopted on 4 October 1983, while the Committee of Ministers adopted it and made it public on 2 April 1992. On the basis of new evidence, the commission affirmed its previous findings that an "indefinite number" of Greek Cypriot missing was in Turkish custody in 1974 in "life threatening conditions." The commission also repeated the presumption of Turkish responsibility (paragraph 117) and expressed "grave concern" that no information had been made available by Turkey to the families of the missing. This failure to account for the fate of persons in Turkish custody was a serious violation of Article 5 of the European Convention, as it caused suffering to the families of the missing. The commission could not exclude that some of the missing may have been killed, but it could not make any definitive findings on the circumstances of their death. The commission also concluded that there was no justification for Turkey to detain any of the missing. Thus, by a vote of

16-1, Turkey was found guilty of violating Article 5 (right to liberty and security of the person) of the European Convention.

The historic decision on 10 May 2001 of the European Court of Human Rights on the fourth Cypriot interstate application against Turkey found Turkey guilty of continuing violations of the European Convention on the issue of the missing. By a vote of 16-1, with the negative vote always being that of the Turkish judge, Turkey was found guilty of violating Article 2 (right to life) by failing to conduct effective investigations of persons who disappeared while in Turkish custody and under life threatening circumstances. By a similar vote, the court determined that Turkey violated Article 5 of the convention (right to liberty and security of the person) by failing to effectively investigate the fate of the missing who had been in its custody. By another vote of 16-1, the court also found Turkey in violation of Article 3 of the convention (inhuman treatment). This part of the decision commented on the agony of the relatives of the missing. The silence of the Turkish authorities "attained a level of severity which can only be categorized as inhuman treatment within the meaning of article 3" (paragraph 157).

In addition to Turkey's specific violations of the European Convention, the court's rationale raised additional substantive points on the missing. It recalled the findings on the missing in the first three Cypriot interstate applications that were handled by the European Commission of Human Rights. Special attention was paid to Turkey's presumption of responsibility for the fate of persons in its custody. The charge of the court was not to establish what happened to those missing since 1974, but to determine whether Turkey's failure to clarify facts surrounding these disappearances constituted a continuing violation of the convention. As shown, Turkey was found guilty of such continuing violations. In another important conclusion, the court determined that its examination of the issue of the missing was not precluded by the work in Cyprus of the Committee on Missing Persons. This was due to the fact that the CMP's scope of work was limited to determining whether the missing were dead or alive. Moreover, the CMP was not empowered to make findings as to the cause of death of the missing persons, or to find the party or parties responsible for such deaths. Further, the CMP's territorial jurisdiction was limited to Cyprus. It excluded investigations in Turkey, and the CMP was not authorized to investigate actions by Turkish officials and army personnel committed on Cypriot soil. According to the European Court of Human Rights, Turkey had a positive obligation to conduct effective investigations of its own, and that was not compensated by the work of the CMP. Paragraph 135 of the court's opinion is explicit on this issue. The respondent, that is, the government of Turkey, could not be discharged by contributing to the work of the CMP, because the CMP's mode of operation was not sufficient to meet the standard of an effective investigation under Article 2 of the European Convention. This important ruling by the European Court of Human Rights reflected not only on Turkey's responsibility but also on the effectiveness of the main instrument created by the United Nations to address the important issue of the missing.

On the Basis of available evidence, in 1990 nine families of missing persons filed cases against Turkey in the European Court of Human Rights.[8] In a collective judgment listed as the case of *Varnava and Others v. Turkey*, on

10 January 2008, by a vote of 6-1, the negative vote being that of the Turkish judge, the court found Turkey guilty of violating the convention in the case of the Cypriot missing. The court found:

- violations of Article 2 of the convention (failure to conduct an effective investigation on the nine who disappeared under life-threatening circumstances);
- a continuing violation of Article 3 (inhuman or degrading treatment in respect to the relatives of the missing because of the lack of information about the missing persons); and
- a continuing violation of Article 5 (right of liberty and security of the person and failure to conduct an investigation in the case of the nine who were deprived of their liberty).

As a result of these violations, the court ordered Turkey to pay monetary damages to the families of the nine missing persons.

International Response to Turkey's Noncompliance

Over the last ten years, the UN Security Council has considered the issue of the missing twice a year, as part of its renewal of the mandate of the UN peacekeeping force in Cyprus. Security Council resolutions routinely call[9] for "urgency" in addressing the humanitarian issue of the missing and for "cooperation" with the Committee on Missing Persons, and have welcomed recent positive developments in the work of the committee. However, these resolutions have failed to account for the decisions of European regional organizations and have not joined in European calls for Turkey's compliance with the decisions of the European Court of Human Rights or the resolutions by the European Parliament and by the Consultative Assembly of the Council of Europe. The reason can be traced back to comments made earlier in this volume about the role of the United States and Great Britain in protecting Turkey from any possible condemnation or sanction for its actions in Cyprus. This is also one of the reasons why the United States has steadfastly argued that the issue of the missing is purely humanitarian and should not be "politicized."

In comparison to the Security Council, the UN General Assembly has been more constructive on the issue of the missing and has adopted various resolutions,[10] starting in 1975. These resolutions called on the secretary-general to exert every effort to trace and account for those missing as a result of the armed conflict between Cyprus and Turkey. Later, on 16 December 1977, the General Assembly asked the secretary-general to set up a committee to trace the fate of the missing. This became the Committee on Missing Persons, whose limited mandate has been described above. Subsequent resolutions have called on the parties to facilitate the work of the CMP and recommended that the Working Group on Enforced and Involuntary Disappearances of the UN Commission on Human Rights assist the CMP to overcome procedural and other problems that plagued its work well into the 1990s.

The issue of the missing also became the subject of discussions in the UN Commission of Human Rights which led to the adoption of a number of resolutions.[11] These resolutions included the right of families to know the fate of their loved ones without delay. In a report dated 8 February 2006, entitled "Study of the Right to the Truth," the UN High Commissioner for Human Rights affirmed the inalienable right to the truth, and that failure to inform families about the fate of missing persons amounted to torture and ill treatment, which was prohibited. The commissioner's report also referred to the European Parliament's resolution of 11 January 1983 on the issue of the missing, on the right of families to know, and on the judgment of the European Court of Human Rights of 10 May 2001 on the fourth Cypriot interstate application in the case of the missing.

The European Commission of Human Rights and the European Court of Human Rights are part of the institutional framework of the Council of Europe. The Parliamentary Assembly of the Council of Europe has also actively followed Turkey's failure to comply with the decisions of both institutions. On 31 March 1987, the Parliamentary Assembly adopted a report by M. Riesen and A. Muller on the refugees and missing in Cyprus. That report upheld the right of families to know the truth about the missing persons. The report's conclusions were incorporated in Recommendation 1056 of 5 March 1987 that was adopted by the Parliamentary Assembly. Two additional recommendations were addressed to the Committee of Ministers referring to the implementation of the decisions of the European Court of Human Rights. Recommendation 1546 of 22 January 2002 of the Parliamentary Assembly regretted the fact that the Committee of Ministers had not introduced measures to implement the decision of the European Court of Human Rights (paragraph 3) as it had recommended earlier. In Recommendation 1576 of 23 September 2002, the assembly specifically called on the Committee of Ministers to take "all necessary measures" to ensure the execution of the court's decisions by Turkey without delay. Even though the recommendation focused on Turkey's noncompliance in the Loizidou case, which will be discussed in the next chapter, the message to the ministers was wider and clear. The Committee of Ministers could not continue to tolerate a situation where a respondent state was in breach of its obligations under the European Convention.

The European Parliament, which is the legislative organ of the European Union, has also taken up the issue of the Cypriot missing. In an 11 January 1983 resolution, the European Parliament recognized the right of the families of the missing to know about the fate of their loved ones and declared that delays in addressing this issue impeded an early and peaceful solution to the Cyprus problem (paragraph 6). Another important conclusion (Paragraph 5) stated that the enjoyment of human rights and fundamental freedoms in Cyprus would not be possible until all foreign forces were withdrawn. A resolution adopted on 10 March 1988 linked the consequences of Turkey's actions in Cyprus not only to the UN Charter but also to the Helsinki Final Act. Paragraphs 7 and 8 specifically addressed the issue of the missing, the right of families to know, and the need for the release of any persons who may still be detained by Turkey. On 12 September 1991, the European Parliament declared "incomprehensible"(paragraph 1) the lack of EU involvement in Cyprus in view of the issues at stake. Cyprus was an associate of the EU at the time. The preamble of the resolution also noted that nearly 2,000 persons were missing in Cyprus. Finally, a resolution adopted on 27 March 1996 reminded that Cyprus was headed for EU membership. It condemned statements by Turkish Cypriot leader Rauf Denktash that Turkish Cypriot forces had killed the Greek Cypriot missing. The resolution found these acts to be in violation of the 1949 Geneva Conventions and demanded that Turkey account in "honesty and good faith" for the fate of the missing.

Chapter three discussed the conflicts created by the multiple roles performed by the members of the Committee of Ministers. As the political organ responsible for the implementation of the judgments of the European Court of Human Rights, the Committee of Ministers has often placed political, security, and economic priorities ahead of its responsibility to promote and protect human rights. This is why both the Parliamentary Assembly of the Council of Europe and the European Parliament have recently shown their frustration with the conduct of the Council of Ministers and have increased the public pressure for a change in that behavior in order to fulfill the objectives of both the European Convention and the European Union. Slowly, the Committee of Ministers began responding to these pressures. In its interim resolution DH (2005) 44, concerning the judgment of the European Court of Human Rights of 10 May 2001 on the fourth Cypriot interstate application against Turkey, the Committee of Ministers on 7 June 2005:

- found that the court had determined fourteen violations of the convention by Turkey since the 1974 "Turkish military intervention";
- recalled Turkey's obligation to comply with court judgments under Article 46 (para. 1) of the convention, to adopt measures to end such violations, to erase the consequences of the said violations, and to prevent new violations similar to the ones determined by the court;
- found the need for such measures "pressing" in view of the elapsed time;
- made specific references to the issue of the missing and to the living conditions of the Greek Cypriots enclaved in the occupied areas;
- agreed with the court on the absence of effective investigation of the fate of the missing by Turkey and declared that the CMP procedures were neither sufficient nor adequate to meet the standard of effective investigation;
- called on Turkey to facilitate the work of the CMP and that, if no convincing results were achieved in the "near future," Turkey must take measures to bring about an effective investigation on the missing; and
- asked Turkey to intensify efforts to bring about a full and complete execution of the court's judgment in the fourth Cypriot interstate application, including the issue of the missing. Until Turkey took all necessary measures, the Committee of Ministers would keep the issue of the implementation of the court's decision under review.

Even though it welcomed the progress made by the CMP in Cyprus, the Committee of Ministers again called on Turkey on 10 April 2007 to inform the committee on additional measures taken to facilitate the work of the CMP and to fulfill the court's decision. Turkey has not been responsive to the calls by the Committee of Ministers.

This discussion points to the slow progress made in resolving one of the most tragic consequences of the Turkish invasion and the motives behind the slow implementation of the decisions of the commission and the court. It also points to the growing frustration of European legislative organs with the European political process and shows the evolving political power of these legislative institutions. These institutions are now demanding political accountability by the Committee of Ministers. The evolution of the European Union and the European human rights regime has had a lot to do with this positive development. As shown in chapter two, European human rights institutions deliberately followed a conservative path in asserting their powers under the European Convention, powers that challenged traditional notions of sovereignty.

Despite progress in the work of the CMP, the issue of the missing remains an open wound in Cypriot society and will remain so until Turkey provides:

- complete lists of the Greek Cypriot POWs and other detainees transported to Turkey, beyond the names included on the ICRC repatriation lists;
- complete accounting of persons listed on ICRC documents but not repatriated;
- information on POWs and other detainees transported to Turkey before the activation of the ICRC;
- military reports and records of the Turkish army on the numbers of persons transported to Turkey and detained in Turkish jails;
- any documents on Greek Cypriot battlefield casualties and the number of POWs killed and detained in 1974;
- information on POWs and other detainees in Turkish jails transferred for medical treatment; and
- photographs of all Greek Cypriots transported to Turkey. The Turkish authorities took two photos of each person under their control.

Turkey's obligation to comply with rulings of the European Court of Human Rights can no longer be avoided. The issue of the missing remains a major humanitarian and political issue. Turkey's legal and political obligations will not go away, especially as Turkey seeks closer integration with the EU. The issues of the missing and the enforcement of the decisions of the European Court of Human Rights are one more example why Cyprus has become a major testing ground of the priority given to the rule of law, democracy, and human rights in post-Cold War Europe.

The Enclaved

This section examines the fate and violations of the human rights of another group of Cypriots, Greek and Maronite, a group known as the "enclaved." In the aftermath of the Turkish invasion, some twenty thousand Greek and Maronite Cypriots living in the area that came under Turkish military control refused to leave their villages. The group included many persons living in the Karpass Peninsula of northeast Cyprus and the Maronite villages and townships west of the city of Kyrenia. Their hope was that, following the ceasefire, they would be able to remain in their homes and continue with their lives. They were proven wrong. They soon became victims of Turkey's ethnic cleansing policies. Through oppression, harassment, denial of educational opportunities or access to medical care, restrictions in their freedom of movement and their religious rights, and violations of their home, family, and privacy rights, their number has now been reduced to approximately 504 persons. This includes 378 Greek and 126 Maronite Cypriots.[12] The fate of the enclaved provides one more example of Turkey's policy of discrimination. The actions directed against the enclaved were carried out because of their ethnicity, religion, and language.

According to reports by the UN secretary-general to the UN Security Council, the largest drop in the numbers of the enclaved occurred between September 1974 and December 1976, when their numbers were reduced from approximately 20,000 to 3,631 Greek Cypriots and 776 Maronite Cypriots. Ten years after the invasion these numbers were further reduced to 844 and 377, respectively. Since then, the numbers of the enclaved have continued to decline to their present levels. With an average age of about 70, statistically, this population is likely to disappear in another decade if the current political stalemate continues and no Greek or Maronite Cypriots are allowed to voluntarily return to their homes in peace and safety.

A Personal Experience

In the fall of 2005 and spring of 2006 I traveled to the Karpass Peninsula and the Maronite village of Kormakitis. In the Karpass Peninsula I witnessed the tragic living conditions of the enclaved. I followed an UNFICYP convoy bringing basic food and relief supplies to the enclaved from the free areas of Cyprus. Turkish Cypriot police, who shadowed the UN convoy, kept a record of the supplies given to the enclaved and monitored the interaction of the enclaved with UNFICYP personnel. In the year 2005 this was an unforgettable sight, considering that it was happening on the territory of an EU member, territory occupied since 1974 by a country aspiring to become an EU member. On the way to the historic monastery of Apostolos Andreas, on the easternmost point of the island, I came across wild herds of donkeys running free in the open fields. They appeared to be the only free beings in that beautiful, desolate, occupied land.

The Third Vienna Agreement (1975)

On 2 August 1975, at the conclusion of the third round of UN-sponsored intercommunal talks in Vienna, an agreement was reached between the leaders of the Greek and Turkish Cypriot communities. Known as the "Third Vienna Agreement,"[13] it contained important provisions about the enclaved:

- Greek Cypriots at present in the north of the island were free to stay. They would be given help to lead a normal life. This included facilities for education and the practice of religion, as well as medical care by their own doctors, and freedom of movement in the north.
- Greek Cypriots residing in the north who, at their own request and without having been subjected to any kind of pressure, wished to move south would be permitted to do so.
- UNFICYP would have free and normal access to Greek Cypriot villages and habitations in the north.
- Priority would be given to the reunification of families which may also involve the transfer of a number of Greek Cypriots at present in the south to the north.

As it will be shown in this section, despite the terms of this agreement, Turkey and the surrogate Turkish Cypriot authorities have violated all of its terms. This is why the numbers of the enclaved have reached the lows mentioned above.

The Case of the Maronite Cypriots

Because of its geographic proximity to Lebanon and Syria, Cyprus has, for several hundred years, been home to a Maronite community. Originating primarily in Lebanon, they practice the Maronite version of Catholicism, speak their own Arabic dialect, use the Aramaic language in their liturgy, and have their own culture and customs. Fluent in Greek, for constitutional purposes the Maronites chose to be counted as part of the Greek Cypriot community under the terms of the 1960 constitution. The same was true for Cypriots of Armenian and Latin heritage. About 98 percent of the nearly 6,000 Maronite Cypriots currently live in the free areas of the republic. Most of the major Maronite villages, including Kormakitis, Asomatos, and Karpasia, are in the Kyrenia district of occupied Cyprus. The Maronite village of Ayia Marina is in the occupied section of the Nicosia district. Most of the Maronite inhabitants of these villages have been forced to leave, as their homes, schools, warehouses, and other facilities have been taken over by the Turkish Army or have become part of Turkish military districts with severe restrictions in the movement of the original inhabitants. The Maronite Cypriots have also become victims of Turkey's ethnic cleansing policies that aim to turkify the occupied part of Cyprus.

The Enclaved: Choosing to Stay—Choosing to Leave

A recent study on the enclaved[14] examined the reasons why they chose to leave their homes for the safety of the government-controlled areas. Reasons included:

- the repressive tactics of the occupation authorities applied on the enclaved, including rapes, beatings, restrictions in their freedom of movement, difficulties in obtaining permits to cultivate their fields, cutting off electricity and water supplies, fear of free expression, and various threats;
- the need to reunite families in conditions of freedom and safety;
- inability to communicate with the free areas due to restrictions on the use of telephones and the lack of electronic or regular mail communication;
- health conditions and the lack of adequate medical care, particularly serious because of the average age of the enclaved population;
- anxiety and uncertainty of parents for their children. Children over the age of twelve had to attend school in the free areas away from their parents and without the ability to communicate with them. This was a very important issue, given the nature of Cypriot society and the close-knit family structure. Children over the age of sixteen for boys and eighteen for girls were prohibited from returning to their homes after their studies, even for a visit;
- economic conditions due to the lack of adequate employment, being forced to sell their products at lower than market prices, inability to provide for the future of their children, and restrictions in cultivating their fields;
- immovable property could not be bequeathed to relatives living in the free areas of Cyprus; and
- the pressures created on the enclaved by the arrival of Anatolian settlers from mainland Turkey.

Those who chose to stay, despite the oppressive conditions that drove the others to the safety of the government-controlled areas, did so because of:

- love of their land and home;
- fear and uncertainty of becoming displaced and abandoning their possessions;
- food, financial, and humanitarian assistance provided from the government of the Republic of Cyprus; and
- hope that a solution to the Cyprus problem would improve their living conditions.

The Life of an Enclaved Person

Over the years and prior to the partial lifting of the restrictions along the ceasefire line by the occupation forces on 23 April 2003, the enclaved lived lives of misery, fear, and intimidation. These conditions were created with the deliberate intent of forcing the few remaining Greek and Maronite Cypriots from their ancestral homes. These intentional actions were directed at the enclaved because of their ethnicity, language, and religion. In addition to the acts of commission or omission by the occupation forces and the surrogate regime of the occupied areas, settlers from the Turkish mainland were also used to create conditions of fear and intimidation.

Living conditions for the enclaved have somewhat improved since 23 April 2003. The daily presence of Greek Cypriot and foreign visitors in the occupied areas and the moderation of some of the policies of the occupation regime have provided temporary relief for the enclaved. However, the violations of their rights continue. What form did these violations take?

- During the course of the invasion, men, women, and children of all ages were detained under inhuman conditions with deprivation of food, water, and medical care. Many were held as hostages until the military operations ended.
- Once the ceasefire had taken effect, the enclaved lived under strict daily curfew.
- The movement of the enclaved was restricted to one kilometer from their home unless they received permission to move to the government-controlled areas.
- The enclaved were not allowed to visit friends or other family members in the occupied areas.
- Special permission was required to work in one's own field, and when such permission was granted it was done under degrading conditions and complicated procedures. This affected the livelihood of the enclaved because they were primarily farmers.
- The total disruption of their economic life drove most of the enclaved either to the safety of the government-controlled areas or made them dependent on the limited humanitarian assistance allowed from the government of the Republic of Cyprus. This assistance was delivered through UNFICYP, despite the provisions of the Third Vienna Agreement (1975).
- Persons who had been detained by the occupation authorities during the course of the invasion had to present themselves twice daily to the local police, where they were treated in a degrading manner.
- The enclaved lived under the continuous supervision of the occupation regime. The few allowed to use public telephones did so in the presence of Turkish Cypriot police, while the privacy of their correspondence was not respected.

- Enclaved of all ages were indiscriminately abused, beaten, arrested, or jailed for reasons such as not saluting a member of the occupation army.
- Searches of persons and homes continued indiscriminately, even during the night.
- Assault and battery was a common occurrence, and the incidents of terror tactics increased with the arrival of Anatolian settlers from Turkey. The enclaved had no effective local remedies or protection against such abuses.
- Denial of medical care by Greek Cypriot physicians who could communicate with their patients. Those sent to the free areas for medical treatment were not allowed to return to their homes and families.
- The separation of families and the disruption of family life started with the expulsion of Greek Cypriots from the occupied areas. Separation of families continued under the oppressive tactics already mentioned.
- The enclaved needed escorts to go to church or the market. More often than not, such escorts were not available, so the enclaved could not carry on with their lives.
- Until 2003, education was limited to a few poorly equipped and staffed elementary schools. Books used by these students came from the free areas of the republic. They were heavily censored and the few teachers assigned to teach the elementary students had to be approved by the occupation authorities.
- The practice of religion was also restricted by a combination of methods involving the destruction, looting, and desecration of churches, limitations on religious activities (including the old Ottoman practice of banning the ringing of church bells), and limitations on the freedom of movement of the few remaining priests and parishioners.
- There were instances of forced labor.
- There was no access to media of any type from the free areas of the republic.
- In addition to property confiscation, enclaved persons leaving the occupied areas lost some of their movable and all of their immovable property. Property could not be bequeathed to the families of the enclaved living in the free areas of Cyprus. This was another ethnic cleansing tactic forcibly changing property ownership patterns and creating ethnically homogeneous areas.

In addition to the absence of, or access to, effective local remedies for the enclaved, UNFICYP also faced severe restrictions in its operations despite the terms of its deployment in Cyprus and the provisions of the 1975 Third Vienna Agreement. UNFICYP was not allowed to establish observation posts in the occupied areas of Cyprus or to carry out patrols to ensure the safety and security of the enclaved. It should be noted that UNFICYP performed these tasks routinely on behalf of the Turkish Cypriots who chose to remain in the free areas of the republic after 1975. All UN convoys bringing food supplies and other humanitarian assistance to the enclaved did so under strict rules, while all contact with the enclaved was closely monitored by Turkish Cypriot authorities.

The European Court of Human Rights and the Fate of the Enclaved

The conditions described above constituted major violations of the European Convention. Previous chapters have documented the findings in the first three interstate applications filed by Cyprus against Turkey. The decisions on these applications documented among other violations the forcible expulsion of Greek Cypriots from the occupied area, the separation of families, the deprivations of possessions, forced labor, the lack of effective remedies, and wanton killings.

Two recent cases at the European Court of Human Rights addressed serious violations of human rights under the convention in the case of the enclaved. The first was the historic European Court of Human Rights decision of 10 May 2001 on the fourth interstate application by Cyprus against Turkey. By 16 votes to 1, the negative vote being that of the Turkish judge, the court:

- held that there was a continuing violation of Article 9 of the convention involving the freedom of thought, conscience, and religion because of the restrictive practices applied on the enclaved. This included restrictions that prevented the organization of Greek Orthodox religious ceremonies in a normal and regular manner, the refusal to approve the appointment of priests, restrictions of access to the historic monastery of Apostolos Andreas, and restrictions on movement resulting in denial of access to places of worship outside the villages of the enclaved;
- determined a continuing violation of Article 10 of the convention on the protection of the freedom of expression. The court decried the excessive censorship applied to elementary school books used by the children of the enclaved;
- determined continuing violations of Article 1, Protocol I of the convention. This involved the peaceful enjoyment of possessions, the confiscation of property of those forced to leave the occupied areas and allocation of such property to third parties, and the refusal to recognize inheritance rights of relatives living in the free areas of the republic;
- determined that there had been a continuing violation of Article 2 of Protocol I of the convention in respect to the children of the enclaved who were denied access to secondary school facilities. As shown earlier, once these children attended school in the free areas, they could not return to their families and home;
- determined continuing violations of Article 3 of the convention. The enclaved had been subjected to discriminatory treatment amounting to degrading treatment. In a series of powerful statements (paragraphs 301, 307, 309, and 310), the court found that the enclaved were compelled to live in a situation of isolation. The Greek Cypriots were controlled and restricted in their movements with no prospect of renewing or developing their community. These conditions were debasing and

violated the very notion of respect for the dignity of the members of that community;

- determined a continuing violation of Article 8 of the convention involving the respect of private and family life and respect for the home. The court noted serious restrictions on the exercise of these rights, monitoring of the movements and contacts of the enclaved, and surveillance and even physical presence of state agents in the homes of Greek Cypriots during social gatherings and family visits; and

- determined a continuing violation of Article 13 of the convention because of the absence of effective remedies. The court qualified this ruling by indicating that access to such remedies would not constitute recognition of the so-called "TRNC" (paragraph 92). The court also concluded that the rule of the exhaustion of available remedies was inapplicable "where an administrative practice, namely a repetition of acts incompatible with the Convention and official tolerance by the state authorities, has been shown to exist and is of such nature as to make proceedings futile or ineffective" (paragraph 99). This was an important ruling with serious implications for the issue of recourse to the Property Compensation Commission set up in the occupied areas intended to address Greek Cypriot property claims. This will be discussed in the next chapter.

The court's powerful statements on the issue of the enclaved leave no doubt as to Turkey's objectives and the consequences of its actions since its 1974 invasion. Turkey's noncooperation with the court and its nonimplementation of the decisions of the European Court of Human Rights will weigh heavily on EU decisions on Turkey's accession negotiations. The European Convention is part of EU law and the obligation of implementing court decisions is unequivocal.

The second case involving the European Court and the rights of the enclaved involves the admissibility decision in the application of Eleni Foka[15] by the Third Section of the European Court of Human Rights on 9 November 2006. The applicant is a Greek Cypriot expelled from the occupied areas. She was mistreated and prevented from returning to her home and her occupation as a teacher in an elementary school for the enclaved children. In addition to her description of the inhuman and degrading treatment she received in the hands of the occupation authorities, Foka argued that these violations occurred because of her ethnic origin, religious beliefs, and opposition to Turkey's military occupation. The court has declared this case admissible. In view of the court's findings in the fourth Cypriot interstate application of 10 May 2001, the applicant's case involves one more instance of the fate of the enclaved.

The International Response to the Fate of the Enclaved

The oppression of the enclaved and the violations of their human rights have also been documented by various other independent observers. For example, in its 1977 report on Cyprus,[16] the German NGO Asme-Humanitas noted the same violations that were included in the Cypriot interstate applications against Turkey. The report similarly concluded that the living conditions of the enclaved worsened with the influx of settlers from the Turkish mainland.

In his 12 February 2004 report to the Committee of Ministers and to the Parliamentary Assembly on his visit to Cyprus,[17] the Council of Europe's commissioner for human rights, Alvaro Gil-Robles, summarized violations of the convention ascribable to Turkey. These violations have also been documented by organs of the Council of Europe and the European Court of Human Rights. Gil-Robles notes that, despite improvements in the condition of the enclaved since the partial lifting of the restrictions along the ceasefire line, the problems noted by the court persist. He concluded that the way for the future is "respect for others, not their annihilation."

In a similar report to the Parliamentary Assembly of the Council of Europe, which included a draft resolution dated 20 February 2003,[18] Swiss rapporteur Dick Marty endorsed the conclusions of the European Court of Human Rights in the decision of 10 May 2001 on the fourth Cypriot interstate application against Turkey in the case of the enclaved. Resolution 1333 (2003) and the report by Dick Marty reminded that Turkey was obligated to secure and respect human rights under the convention for all persons in the territory controlled by the Turkish Cypriot "administration." The rapporteur was "extremely concerned" by the status of the enclaved Greek and Maronite Cypriots. He was "particularly shocked" by the imposed division of families, the prohibition on the right of young persons to return home, expropriation of property, and conditions of fear and apprehension among the enclaved. Earlier resolutions by the Parliamentary Assembly[19] expressed the assembly's great concern about the violations of human rights of the enclaved and asked the Committee of Ministers to take "all necessary measures" to convince Turkey to implement the court decision.

In turn, the European Parliament, the legislative organ of the European Union, adopted its own series of relevant resolutions:

- On 27 March 1996, it deplored the refusal of the "occupation regime" to allow a subcommittee of the European Parliament to visit and examine the living conditions of the enclaved, and demanded that Turkey take all necessary measures to facilitate this visit.
- On 24 October 1996, a resolution noted the continuing violations of the rights of the enclaved, including the right to education. It, too, called on Turkey to implement fully the 1975 Third Vienna Agreement.
- On 10 April 1997, a resolution adopted by the European Parliament provided a detailed and damning indictment of the violations of human rights of the enclaved and reminded Turkey of its violation of the Third Vienna Agreement.
- On 15 November 2000, the European Parliament linked Turkey's progress toward EU accession with its compliance and implementation of "previous and future" European Court of Human Rights decisions.

Earlier sections of this and the previous chapter have indicated the growing frustration of the members of the Parliamentary Assembly of the Council of

Europe with the Committee of Ministers' reluctance to enforce judgments against Turkey, and with Turkey's noncooperation with European institutions. Turkey's EU aspirations finally stimulated a resolution by the Committee of Ministers[20] concerning the implementation of the 10 May 2001 judgment of the court. This resolution reiterated the court's findings on the enclaved, encouraged Turkey to continue lifting restrictive measures against the enclaved, and called for the "full and complete execution of the present judgment." The Committee of Ministers decided to continue monitoring Turkey "until all necessary measures are taken."

For reasons already discussed, the UN Security Council has been more circumspect in its criticism of Turkey's conduct on the issue of the enclaved. A number of provisions on the enclaved have been incorporated in recent resolutions, particularly Resolution 1032 (19 December 1995), which endorsed the recommendations made by UNFICYP to improve the conditions of the enclaved. Additional resolutions since then continue to express regret that the Turkish Cypriots, rather than Turkey, have not responded to or implemented the recommendations on the enclaved submitted by UNFICYP.

The Future of the Enclaved

The material presented in this section on the fate of the enclaved and the unequivocal condemnation of Turkey's treatment of these persons leaves no doubt about the serious condition of the rapidly diminishing number of Greek and Maronite Cypriots in the occupied areas. Turkey has nearly succeeded in completing the ethnic cleansing of the occupied areas that began on 20 July 1974. It is a testimony to human endurance that the few hundred remaining enclaved persons have survived persecution, oppression, and inhuman treatment for more than three decades. In June 1995, UNFICYP carried out a review of the living conditions of the enclaved Greek and Maronite Cypriots and made recommendations as to how these conditions can be improved. Details of UNFICYP's recommendations have been included in the 10 December 1995 Report by the secretary-general on the operations of the peacekeeping force in Cyprus.[21] The simple and humane changes proposed by UNFICYP would go a long way toward addressing the restrictive, oppressive, and discriminatory policies of the occupation regime. As shown, the European Court of Human Rights has also condemned these policies. Turkey would have been spared of much of the condemnation by the European Court had these simple suggestions been implemented. Despite the limited improvement in the conditions of the enclaved since the partial lifting of the crossing restrictions along the ceasefire line, the problem of the enclaved remains unresolved. It is one more shameful stigma on the protection of human rights in twenty-first-century Europe.

> The treatment complained of was clearly discriminatory against them on the basis of their "ethnic origin, race and religion." . . . The hardships [to] which the Greek Cypriots were subjected . . . attained a level of severity which constituted an affront to human dignity.[22]

CHAPTER SIX

The Continuing Consequences of Ethnic Cleansing: Property Usurpation, Settlers, and the Destruction of Cultural Heritage

THE PRECEDING two chapters have addressed the human dimension of the consequences of the Turkish invasion and continuing occupation of Cyprus. As the evidence presented shows, the Turkish objective was ethnic cleansing and the creation of two separate and ethnically homogeneous states on the island.

This chapter will focus on how Turkey and its surrogate have gone about altering the social, cultural, economic, and political character of the occupied area and erasing its Hellenic past. The discussion in this chapter centers on the confiscation and usurpation of Greek Cypriot-owned properties, the impact of settlers both on the occupied area and in Cyprus in general, and the systematic destruction of the Greek Cypriot cultural heritage. All three actions have been designed to complete the ethnic cleansing process by erasing any evidence of Greek Cypriot presence and heritage in occupied Cyprus. This chapter will discuss the extent of these problems, the legal aspects of Turkey's actions, and the international response to these documented and continuing violations of European and international law.

Property Issues: From Confiscation to Usurpation

The right to property has been defined as a basic human right in Western jurisprudence as well as in the tradition and practice of Western societies. It was upheld in the 1948 United Nations Universal Declaration of Human Rights (Article 17), it is a basic part of the European Convention (Article 1, Protocol I), and it is one of the fundamental articles in the Charter of Fundamental Rights of the European Union (Article 17). In addition to international and domestic protections of the right to property, Cypriot culture and tradition places significant value on immovable property and land. It is an important part of a family's heritage, roots, and identity. This is why it is a difficult concept to convey to a largely mobile contemporary American public. It was also a point missed by the drafters of the "Annan Plan." They attempted to resolve the difficult property issue primarily through compensation and property exchange, as demanded by Turkey, rather than through restitution, as provided for under international law and preferred by Greek Cypriot refugees and displaced persons. This was one of the many reasons for the plan's rejection by the Greek Cypriot voters in the referendum of 24 April 2004.

Chapter four addressed the documented looting, plundering, and wanton destruction of Greek Cypriot property in the days following the 1974 Turkish invasion. In 1974, prior to the invasion, the land registry records of the Republic of Cyprus showed that 82.5 percent of the privately owned land in the area that came under Turkish occupation was owned by Greek Cypriots. As Greek Cypriots fled for their lives or were expelled by the occupation regime, their properties were confiscated and redistributed to Turkish Cypriots and settlers from the Turkish mainland under regulations promulgated by the occupation regime. The unrecognized "Turkish Federated State of Cyprus" issued various regulations in 1975, as did the unrecognized "Turkish Republic of Northern Cyprus" after 1983. These expropriations were formalized under Article 159 of the "constitution" of the "TRNC" in 1985. The decisions on the interstate applications filed by Cyprus against Turkey at the European Commission of Human Rights, and by Greek Cypriot property owners against Turkey in the European Court of Human Rights, held that acts by unrecognized political entities were invalid and in violation of the European Convention. These violations were imputable to Turkey because of its effective control of occupied Cyprus. These decisions also confirmed the ownership rights of Greek Cypriot displaced and refugees.

Greek Cypriot property owners have been denied access to and enjoyment of their properties since 1974. Moreover, the families of the displaced, the refugees, and the enclaved have lost their inheritance rights to these properties under the usurpation policies of the occupation regime. The land policies adopted in the occupied areas were intended to erase any evidence of Greek Cypriot presence or claim in the occupied areas, one more part of the Turkish strategy of ethnic cleansing.

Despite European Court of Human Rights decisions upholding the ownership rights of Greek Cypriot property owners, the occupation authorities proceeded to issue illegal titles to these properties not only to Turkish Cypriots but also to illegal Turkish settlers as well. In 2002, the occupation authorities went a step further and allowed illegal possessors of stolen Greek Cypriot property to transfer or sell such properties to third parties other than Greek Cypriots. Since then, there has been an unprecedented construction boom in the occupied territories as well as property investments and sales primarily to British, German, and Israeli interests. This is quite evident around the city of Kyrenia, in the historic village of Bellapais, and, increasingly, near the pristine Karpass Peninsula and the coastal areas west of Kyrenia. Natural beauty, a pristine environment, and relatively low prices are driving much of this investment and development.

Another reason for the illegal building boom on property belonging to Greek Cypriot displaced, refugees, and enclaved persons has been the failed UN-sponsored Annan Plan for the resolution of the Cyprus problem. Had the Greek Cypriot voters approved the fifth version of this plan (Annan V), it would have essentially overturned the precedents set by the European Court of

Human Rights in decisions involving Greek Cypriot properties.[1] Pending property cases against Turkey at the European Court of Human Rights would have also been withdrawn. The failed UN plan encouraged illegal property transfers by the occupation regime by severely restricting the right to restitution and by legalizing unlawful property transfers that had taken place. Coupled with the restrictions included in Annan V on two basic freedoms, namely, the right to settlement and property ownership, the former secretary-general's plan would have nullified Greek Cypriot property rights in occupied Cyprus.

The Annan Plan created the impression that unlawful investments by Turks, Turkish Cypriots, and other foreign nationals would be protected, thus removing fears of dealing in stolen property. The massive building activity and usurpation of Greek Cypriot property served various purposes, among which are the following:

- It was intended to discourage attempts by Greek Cypriots to reclaim their properties. The illegal sales and building on Greek Cypriot properties was creating a "new reality" in the occupied areas. Until the partial opening by the occupation forces of the crossing points along the ceasefire line, Greek Cypriot refugees and displaced had no access to the occupied areas. They still have no access to their homes and properties.
- The occupation authority and its surrogate used the distribution and sale of stolen properties to buy off political influence and to create dependence on the occupation regime by settlers and Turkish Cypriots.
- It was a means of attracting badly needed foreign currency and investment to occupied Cyprus.
- It was a Turkish government-sponsored incentive to encourage mainland Turkish settlers to come and settle in occupied Cyprus.
- It was creating a fait accompli intended to prejudice on "humanitarian grounds" any future settlement of the Cyprus problem.

The Politics of "Domestic Remedies"

In an attempt to avoid further negative judgments on property issues by the European Court of Human Rights against Turkey, the occupation regime introduced a "domestic remedies law" in June 2003. This "law" was amended in December 2005 in an attempt to reduce conflicts with international law. This "law"[2] was intended to force Greek Cypriot displaced and refugees to resort to the "Property Commission" of the "TRNC" prior to any recourse to the European Court of Human Rights. It was also part of Turkey's strategy that the issue of property would be solved under a global political settlement through compensation and property exchange and not through cases at the European Court of Human Rights. This was also the thesis guiding the "Annan Plan" and its proposals on property.

There are a number of problems with this political and legal maneuver by Turkey and its occupation regime:

- The European Commission of Human Rights and the European Court of Human Rights in their rulings spoke of the absence of effective local remedies in the occupied areas for aggrieved Greek Cypriots. They also indicated that even if there were local remedies available, especially for the enclaved, access to such remedies did not constitute recognition of this illegal entity. In contrast, Turkey and its "subordinate local administration" saw the establishment of this commission and the utilization of its procedures as one more step in the institutionalization of the "TRNC" and its eventual de facto statehood.
- This "law" was another method of shifting responsibility away from Turkey for the violations of property rights in occupied Cyprus.
- The "law" was intended to satisfy the requirements of Article 35 (par. 1) of the European Convention requiring exhaustion of "domestic remedies" prior to having recourse to the European Court of Human Rights. However, as the court has also ruled, appellants have no such obligation if available remedies are inadequate or ineffective, or if the "national authorities" have failed to investigate misconduct or "state agents" have inflicted harm.
- This "law" remains in conflict with international law. Despite its title, it relies on property compensation and/or property exchange, while effectively precluding the right to property restitution provided for by international law.
- Acceptance of compensation or property exchange would automatically eliminate title to property located in the occupied areas. This was intended to legalize the exclusion of any Greek Cypriot presence in occupied Cyprus which was the objective of Turkey's ethnic cleansing plan.
- For compensation purposes, the value of the property was based on the estimated property value on 20 July 1974, the date of the Turkish invasion, and not at the levels at which usurped Greek Cypriot property was currently selling in the occupied areas.
- The "Property Commission" was not empowered to halt or control the continuing violation of property rights of the Greek Cypriot displaced or refugees.

A largely overlooked issue involves the precedent of Turkey's own compensation law, "With Respect to Internally Displaced People."[3] That law and its procedures have many similarities and parallels to the "law" in effect in occupied Cyprus. The Turkish law devalued and manipulated property values, underestimated land holdings, underestimated or excluded compensation for orchards and other stocks, and limited the persons entitled to compensation. Given that Turkey is in effective control of the occupied areas, this law is not an encouraging precedent. Similar was the experience of the Greek victims of the 1955 Turkish government-sponsored and directed pogrom in Istanbul. The compensation committee set up by the Turkish government to examine claims of the Greek victims of that pogrom set a precedent for the Kurdish victims.

The so-called "domestic remedies" provided by the 2003 "law" and its 2005 amended version had no effect in the implementation of the decision by the European Court of Human Rights by the Committee of Ministers in the case of Loizidou against Turkey, or the Xenidis-Aresti case against Turkey, which will be discussed below in this chapter.

The Extent of Usurpation

The massive scale of the usurpation, expropriation, exploitation, and misappropriation of Greek Cypriot properties has been documented in various ways, including:

- Turkish Cypriot websites and media advertising by realty firms in occupied Cyprus and Great Britain promoting sales and property development.
- the visible evidence (advertising billboards) seen by anyone driving across occupied Cyprus.
- statements on the public record by Turkish Cypriot "officials" and by Turkey's former deputy prime minister and minister of state, Abdullatif Sener, providing comparative sale and construction figures since 2001. These include:
  o the purchase of land by foreign nationals. In 2001 this amounted to 63,000 sq. meters. In 2003 these sales had risen to 613,000 sq. meters.
  o the number of foreign nationals applying to buy property in occupied Cyprus. In 2000 there were 228 applications. In the first nine months of 2004 the number had risen to 701 applications.
  o the value of property sales. In 2004 the amount was estimated at $2 billion.
  o the amount and value of construction materials, mainly iron and cement imported in the occupied areas.[4] Iron imports in the first half of 2004 amounted to 42,335 tons compared to 17,856 tons in all of 2001. Cement imports in 2001 amounted to 50,914 tons, while in 2004 that figure had risen to 106,200 tons.
- the building of hotels and casinos in coveted areas of the island intended to attract tourists primarily from Great Britain, Germany, and Israel. A decision on 26 March 2006 by the so-called "Council of Ministers" of the "TRNC" gave permission for such development in the environmentally pristine and sensitive Karpass Peninsula. Representatives of the government of Turkey play an important role in the committee appointed to guide this development, proving once more Turkey's defining role in the exploitation and usurpation of Greek Cypriot properties. These matters are openly discussed in the Turkish Cypriot daily press, which has provided reliable data on the public loans and incentives offered for such developments. Much of the needed infrastructure work is funded by Turkish financial aid to the occupied areas.

- the dramatic increase in property prices. Former chairman of the Turkish Cypriot Chamber of Commerce Eren Ertanin estimated that immovable property prices doubled between 2003 and 2005. In reading these figures, it must be kept in mind that up to the time of the Turkish invasion, 82.5 percent of the land and immovable property in occupied Cyprus belonged to Greek Cypriots. Recent satellite maps provide additional proof of the usurpation of these properties.

The Response by the Republic of Cyprus

The government of the Republic of Cyprus has taken a number of important steps to protect the property rights of its citizens against the usurpation policies of the occupation regime. Concerned that these violations of European and international law could potentially create a fait accompli and even prejudice the resolution of the Cyprus problem, it has embarked on a major information campaign about the consequences of the unlawful exploitation of Greek Cypriot properties. The government's concern is not unfounded. It is aware of Turkey's position that the all-important property issue can be solved only within the context of a global political solution, primarily through compensation and property exchange, in order to consolidate the two-state solution on Cyprus. This was also how former Secretary-General Kofi Annan approached the issue in his 2004 arbitration plan.

The urgency of the government's response is due not only to the data already presented about property sales and illegal construction but also to the dramatic increase in the influx of settlers from mainland Turkey to occupied Cyprus with the support and encouragement of the occupation authorities. In 2004, some 40,000 new settlers came to the occupied areas, lured by work and property incentives granted by the occupation authorities. The settlers now outnumber the Turkish Cypriots by a 2:1 ratio. In addition, the massive building process has had serious effects on the natural environment of Cyprus, on various archaeological sites, and even on sites suspected to contain remains of Greek Cypriot missing.

With the support of the Republic of Cyprus, Turkey commenced EU accession negotiations on 3 October 2005, despite its actions in Cyprus and its nonrecognition of the Republic of Cyprus. The government of Cyprus has asked that Turkey impose a moratorium on all construction activity in the occupied areas in the absence of consent by the lawful owners of these properties. The government has also asked Turkey to conduct an internationally supervised census profiling the usage of immovable properties belonging to Greek Cypriots. Turkey has not hitherto complied with this request either, confirming once more its contempt for its international obligations.

In a "note verbale" dated 5 December 2006 by the Ministry of Foreign Affairs to all diplomatic missions accredited to the Republic of Cyprus, the government informed these missions of amendments to the Cypriot criminal code. The amendments covered fraudulent deals in immovable property, including the sale, rent, mortgage, advertising, or accepting such properties without the lawful consent of the registered owner of that property. Such actions amounted to a felony involving a multi-year sentence upon conviction. The amendments to the criminal code became necessary because of the magnitude of the problem that developed in occupied Cyprus and in order to protect property rights under Article 23 of the Constitution of the Republic of Cyprus, and under Article 1, Protocol I to the European Convention. The law applied to all offenses committed against immovable property situated anywhere in the Republic of Cyprus, regardless of where the offense was committed, and regardless of the identities of the lawful owner and the wrong doer.

The government also undertook a massive information campaign, both written and on the internet, cautioning foreign buyers about the risks of buying property in occupied Cyprus. Foreign nationals have also been warned of violations of Cypriot law by the importation into the free areas of material advertising stolen properties. Such confiscated material and the persons carrying it could provide evidence in future cases against property usurpers. Cypriot ambassadors have also communicated with influential media in the country of their accreditation explaining the risks and the law regarding illegal property purchases.[5]

These efforts were complemented by the information campaign of the Cyprus Chapter of the International Real Estate Federation. It informed federation members, under the code of ethics, about the dangers inherent in immovable property transactions in areas not under the control of the government of the republic. An information bulletin, dated 26 May 2006, advised members of the precedent-setting decisions of the European Court of Human Rights in the Loizidou and Xenidis-Aresti cases, informed them of the fact that cases can be brought against usurpers of property in Cypriot courts, and that Cypriot court decisions can be enforced in other jurisdictions as well. Under the law, European arrest warrants can be issued against persons dealing in illegal properties. The Orams case, which will be discussed in the next section, is a classic example. These were not empty threats or political propaganda on the part of the Republic of Cyprus. They constituted a reasoned response intended to address the realities developing in occupied Cyprus.

Interstate Applications and Court Judgments

Aspects of the property issue were included in the decisions of the European Commission of Human Rights and the European Court of Human Rights in all four Cypriot interstate applications against Turkey.

In the report on the first two Cypriot applications,[6] the European Commission on Human Rights found that there was proof that Greek Cypriot property and land were taken by Turkish Cypriots and settlers from mainland Turkey (paragraph 472). There was also evidence that robbery and extensive looting had occurred. These actions, committed against Greek Cypriots, were in violation of Article 14 of the convention (paragraph 503) and imputable to Turkey. Similarly, the European Commission of Human Rights found no evidence of effective and sufficient remedies available to the aggrieved Greek Cypriots (paragraphs 499-501).

In the report on the third Cypriot interstate application,[7] the commission found Turkey in violation of Article 1, Protocol I of the convention (right to property). The commission also noted that the government of Turkey did not dispute the property takeover (paragraphs 152-155). These violations were therefore imputable to Turkey. The commission also found that available remedies were neither relevant nor sufficient and, therefore, did not have to be exhausted by aggrieved Greek Cypriots before bringing claims against the occupation authorities (paragraph 157). The European Commission of Human Rights also concluded that Turkey's actions directed at Greek Cypriots were in violation of the nondiscrimination provisions of the European Convention (paragraph 161).

The historic decision of 10 May 2001 by the European Court of Human Rights on the fourth Cypriot interstate application against Turkey[8] was even more detailed and explicit than the decisions of the European Commission of Human Rights. This decision reaffirmed that:

- the government of the Republic of Cyprus is the sole legitimate government of Cyprus (paragraphs 61, 90);
- the "TRNC" is not a "state" under international law, hence illegal (paragraphs 61, 90, 236, 238);
- the government of Turkey is in effective control and therefore responsible for securing all human rights under the convention. Any violations by agents of Turkey or by the local "administration" were imputable to Turkey (paragraphs 77, 81); and
- the remedies available by the local "administration" were regarded as remedies of Turkey (paragraph 102) and did not amount to recognition, implied or otherwise, of the "TRNC's" claim to statehood (paragraph 238).

Addressing specifically the issue of homes and properties, the European Court of Human Rights noted:

- the continuing violations of the rights of the displaced (Article 8 of the convention) who could not return to their homes and properties and who were physically prevented from even visiting their homes (paragraph 172);
- that the ongoing intercommunal talks or the need to house displaced Turkish Cypriots (paragraph 188) could not be invoked to legitimate a violation of the convention (paragraph 174) involving Greek Cypriot properties;
- the denial of access by displaced Greek Cypriots to their property violated Article 1, Protocol I to the European Convention (paragraph 188); and
- that Greek Cypriots not residing in the occupied areas had no access to effective remedies in order to contest interferences with their rights to property and respect for their homes (paragraphs 193-194). This was a clear violation of Article 13 of the convention.

In addition to the decisions on the four Cypriot interstate applications against Turkey, there are at least four major court decisions involving property issues. The European Court of Human Rights handled three of these cases. The fourth involves Cypriot and British courts. This study has emphasized the importance of legal decisions by European institutions. These decisions provide an important independent record of the consequences of Turkey's invasion. They are based on the European legal order as it evolved since the end of World War II. Consequently, the conclusions included in this discussion are not a product of Cypriot spin masters, but instead reflect European law and provide the foundation for a future political settlement of the Cyprus problem.

The first precedent-setting decision by the European Court of Human Rights involves the *Loizidou v. Turkey* case. The court addressed the issues in this case in three rulings between 1995 and 1998. While the 23 March 1995 ruling dealt with preliminary objections, that of 18 December 1996 addressed the merits of the case. On 28 July 1998 the court ruled on "just satisfaction" issues.

This precedent-setting judgment found Turkey, as an occupying power, to be responsible for the policies and actions of its surrogates in occupied Cyprus. Turkish Cypriot "authorities" were characterized as a "subordinate local administration" of Turkey. Titina Loizidou, a Cypriot citizen from Kyrenia, was denied access to and enjoyment of her property by the occupation authorities. Turkey was found to have violated Article 1 of Protocol I of the European Convention, by its continuing refusal to allow Loizidou access to her property and by the purported expropriation of her property. In the third judgment of 28 July 1998, Turkey was ordered to pay damages to Loizidou amounting to approximately $1.5 million for the nonuse and enjoyment of her property. Loizidou remained the legitimate titleholder of her properties. The absence of effective local remedies was another convention violation that was also noted in the case.

Turkey balked at the penalties imposed by the court and refused to comply. This became an issue that was addressed in resolutions by the Committee of Ministers. It will be discussed in the next section of this chapter. The threat of censure and Turkey's pending application for accession talks with the EU forced the Turkish government to pay the damages granted by the Court in December 2003. However, the issue of the restitution of Loizidou's property remains unresolved. Nevertheless, this precedent-setting case explains:

- the urgency felt by the occupation authorities to adopt a "law" on domestic remedies;
- the financial impact of this decision, given that more than fifty similar cases were pending at the European Court;
- the political pressure Turkey faces because of its noncompliance and continuing violations of the European Convention on the eve of Turkey's accession talks with the EU; and
- the fact that the international community continues to uphold the law and views Turkey as an occupying power, while the actions of the "subordinate local administration" have no legal validity.

The second very important case was that of Myra Xenidis-Aresti against Turkey. This case was filed in 1999. On 6 April 2005, the European Court of Human Rights rendered its decision on the merits of the case, and in December 2006 awarded the applicant pecuniary damages because she was deprived the use and enjoyment of her property in the fenced-in area of Ayios Memnon in Famagusta. The damages included approximately $1.1 million for deprivation of use and enjoyment of her property, nonpecuniary damages of approximately $68,000, and nearly $50,000 for costs and expenses. The court asked Turkey to pay these penalties by 22 August 2007. The Xenidis-Aresti case is important because it upheld:

- the continuing ownership of this property by the applicant, and that the compensation Turkey was ordered to pay was not for the property but for the loss of its use and enjoyment;
- that Turkey committed and continued to commit violations of Article 8 (respect for the home) and Article 1 of Protocol I of the convention (protection of property);
- that these violations occurred because the applicant was a Greek Cypriot which violated the nondiscrimination clause of the convention (Article 14);
- that the domestic remedies available in the occupied areas were neither effective nor adequate. The so-called "Compensation Committee" could not order property restitution, nor could it interfere in the fenced-up area of Famagusta which Turkey considers to be a "military district." Such an area was out of the committee's jurisdiction;
- that the rejection of the Annan Plan for the resolution of the Cyprus problem did not affect the applicant's property rights;
- that Turkey continues to exercise effective overall control of occupied Cyprus and therefore is responsible for human rights violations occurring there; and
- the ongoing intercommunal talks for the resolution of the Cyprus problem do not entail recognition of the "TRNC" or confer to it "statehood."

The European Court of Human Rights applied the same principles in another important Greek Cypriot property case against Turkey, *Demades v. Turkey* (Application No. 16219/90). The "just satisfaction" judgment issued on 22 April 2008 was based on the principles that guided the decisions in the Loizidou and Xenidis-Aresti cases, leaving no doubts as to Turkey's continuing violation of the convention. The applicant was awarded nearly $1.4 million for the non-use and enjoyment of his property, while retaining title to his property.

The fourth important property case involves that of Meletios Apostolides against David and Linda Orams. The case began on 26 October 2004, when the applicant, a Cypriot national, obtained a writ in the Nicosia District Court naming Mr. and Mrs. Orams as defendants, liable for trespass on his property in the occupied area. The Cypriot Court ordered the defendants to demolish the villa and other building erected on the Apostolides property without his permission, to surrender vacant possession to the plaintiff, and to pay damages. Pursuant Regulation 44/2001 of the EU, the judgment of the Nicosia Court could be enforced in any EU member state. The Orams appealed the case to the High Court of Justice—Queens Bench Division in London and were represented by Cherie Booth, QC, wife of the then British prime minister Tony Blair. This was an apparent conflict of interest, as the Blair government was actively involved in the resolution of the Cyprus problem.

In a judgment handed down on 6 September 2006, Justice Black ruled against the defendant, Apostolides, on a technical point, namely, the lack of jurisdiction by the British Court in a case that should be handled by the European Court of Human Rights with Turkey as the defendant. The case is currently on appeal. Justice Black's ruling raised questions as to the applicability of EU rules in occupied Cyprus, a matter that may be decided by the EU's Court of Justice.

Even though this case may not have had the desired outcome, the British judgment is also important because:

- it upheld that the land in the so-called "TRNC" lies within the Republic of Cyprus and, consequently, Cypriot Courts have jurisdiction over all land situated in the republic's territory;
- the Greek Cypriot owners of property in the occupied north remain the owners of their property;
- the so-called "TRNC" cannot deprive legitimate owners of their title to their land; and
- persons buying or occupying land belonging to displaced Greek Cypriots are trespassers and can be treated as such.

All decisions on the four Cypriot interstate applications against Turkey and in the four court cases summarized here are in agreement on the substantive legal issues involved and on Turkey's continuing violations of the European Convention.

The International Response to Court Judgments

On 6 October 1999, the Committee of Ministers of the Council of Europe adopted interim resolution DH (99)680 on the European Court of Human Rights judgment in the Loizidou case. The resolution deplored Turkey's noncompliance and stressed Turkey's obligation to comply with court judgments. In another resolution, DH (2000)105 adopted on 24 July 2000, the Committee of Ministers was even more emphatic. It stated that:

- the obligation to abide by court judgments is unconditional;
- the failure to execute the Loizidou judgment demonstrates a "manifest disregard" by Turkey of its obligations as a High Contracting Party to the convention and as a member of the Council of Europe; and
- the failure by a High Contracting Party to the European Convention to comply with a court judgment is unprecedented.

Turkey was asked to fully comply with the decision without further delay.

Interim resolution DH(2001) 80 of 26 June 2001 went even a step further. Speaking again on the issue of the implementation of the Loizidou judgment, the ministers reiterated the views expressed in their resolution of 24 July 2000, reaffirmed the obligations of Council of Europe members under the convention, and concluded by declaring the Committee of Ministers' resolve to ensure Turkey's compliance "with all means available." As indicated earlier, the public embarrassment and pressures emanating from these resolutions and the pending, at the time, Turkish application for EU accession talks brought the desired result. Turkey made the required penalty payment to Loizidou. These were unprecedented legal and political actions necessary in order to assure compliance by a defiant member. Turkey could not overlook the fact that the members of the Committee of Ministers of the Council of Europe served in the same capacity in the EU and were not likely to forget Turkey's conduct as they reviewed Turkey's case for EU accession talks.

International legal experts and other international conventions addressing property rights of refugees and the displaced uphold the principles we have discussed in this chapter. Alfred de Zayas goes a step further and reminds that both the Fourth Hague Convention of 1907 and the 1949 Geneva Convention (Protocol I of 1977) find illegal all transfers of immovable property to citizens of an occupying power and the usurpation and disposal of such property to third parties illegal. Similar provisions appeared in the Draft Code of "Crimes Against the Peace and Security of Mankind" (1991) and in Article 8 of the Rome Statute of the International Criminal Court (1998).

In his report to the Council of Europe on his 2003 visit to Cyprus, Commissioner for Human Rights Alvaro Gil-Robles noted that, despite the easing by the Turkish authorities of restrictions on the movement across the ceasefire line, Greek Cypriots have not been able to recover or freely dispose of their properties.[9] The commissioner also noted that title deeds issued by the "TRNC" are not recognized by anyone, including the European Court of Human Rights. He further stated that the commission set up in the occupied areas to examine property claims does not enable claimants to recover possession and enjoyment of their properties.

The right of property restitution has also been upheld in resolutions adopted on 11 August 2005 by the Sub-Commission on the Promotion and Protection of Human Rights of the UN Commission of Human Rights.[10] This report reflected on the work of Special Rapporteur Paolo Sergio Pineiro on housing and property restitution in the context of the return of refugees and the internally displaced. In various explanatory notes, the report emphasizes the right to privacy, respect for the home, the peaceful enjoyment of possessions, and the right to voluntarily return to one's own home in safety and dignity. The report goes beyond the principles of the European Convention and outlines rights guaranteed under the Universal Declaration of Human Rights, the International Convention on Civil and Political Rights, and the 1949 Geneva Conventions.

In conclusion, the evidence presented on the violation of Greek Cypriot property rights is based on decisions of independent judicial and political bodies. Turkey's continuing violations were directed at Greek Cypriots because of their ethnicity, language, and religion. These violations have not stopped. No political settlement that violates fundamental principles of European and international law is likely to be accepted by the Greek Cypriots.

The Settlers

"The arrival and establishment of Turkish settlers is the most notable demographic occurrence in Cyprus since 1974." This is how Alfons Cuco, rapporteur of the Committee on Migration, Refugees and Demography of the Parliamentary Assembly of the Council of Europe, described the demographic situation in Cyprus.[11] While in 1974 the Turkish Cypriot population was estimated at 114,000, this number has currently dropped to approximately 82,000. The outflow of indigenous Turkish Cypriots is largely due to:

- economic conditions prevailing in the occupied areas;
- social, cultural, economic, and political pressures generated by the influx of settlers, currently estimated at 160,000; and
- social and political conditions created by the presence of over 40,000 Turkish troops in occupied Cyprus.

In 2006, the Turkish Cypriot authorities projected the population of the occupied areas to be approximately 240,000 persons, showing an unusual increase of 31.7 percent in ten years. In simple terms, the settlers outnumbered the native Turkish Cypriots by a ratio of 2:1, a ratio that does not include members of the Turkish occupation army. In his report to the Parliamentary Assembly of the Council of Europe, Alfons Cuco addressed the demographic impact of the Turkish army in occupied Cyprus by indicating that, at a minimum, the ratio of one soldier to six civilians is unique to Europe (paragraph 112). A similar report on 24 June 2003 to the Parliamentary Assembly of the Council of Europe by Rapporteur J. Laakso confirmed Cuco's findings and conclusions.

Both reports conclude that the Turkish settlers are neither "seasonal workers" nor former inhabitants that left Cyprus prior to 1974. These persons have been brought into occupied Cyprus by the government of Turkey and its subordinate local administration with explicit political objectives. This is confirmed by the 1975 "Naturalization Act" adopted by the Turkish Cypriot "administration," and by the 1981 regulations supplementing that act. A protocol, signed on 12 October 2004 between the government of Turkey and its subordinate local administration in occupied Cyprus, allowed all Turkish nationals present in occupied Cyprus without the permission of the Turkish Cypriot authorities to receive residence and work permits. Thus, in 2004 alone, the year of the referendum on the Annan Plan, some 40,000 illegal Turkish settlers entered occupied Cyprus. These figures have been confirmed by reports in the Turkish Cypriot press. Another indicator of the influx and naturalization of settlers is the radical increase in the number of registered voters in the occupied areas. While in 1976, prior to the mass exodus by the Turkish Cypriots, that number was estimated at 75.781 persons, in June 2006 it had doubled to 151,635. According to Turkish Cypriot media, dramatic increases in the numbers of registered voters were noted prior to each election in the occupied area, indicating the political impact of the settlers in the life of occupied Cyprus.

The settlers were provided with various government-sponsored incentives to move to Cyprus including employment, housing and property, citizenship, and full political rights in the unrecognized "TRNC." According to Turkish Cypriot daily *Avrupa* (26 March 2001), by the end of 2000, some 34,000 title deeds had been given to settlers, most of which were titles to usurped Greek Cypriot properties. Since 2002, these titles can be sold to third parties for a handsome profit.

The major influx of settlers noted in 2004 was related to the Annan Plan, which essentially legalized nearly all settlers and opened the way to additional legal arrivals into the proposed "United Cyprus Republic" through the Turkish Cypriot constituent state. The accession of the Republic of Cyprus to the EU was an additional colonization incentive. "Legalized" Turkish settlers in occupied Cyprus would have access to EU and U.S. financial aid (estimated at E275 million annually), employment opportunities in the free areas of the republic, and the possibility of legal migration to other EU states with travel documents from the Republic of Cyprus or its successor state.

The Objectives and Impact of Turkey's Colonization Policy

The Turkish presence in Cyprus was the result of the colonization that followed the Ottoman conquest of the island after 1571 A.D. Settlers and military personnel created the original Turkish minority on the island. The same is the case with today's second Turkish colonization of Cyprus. The colonization sponsored by the Turkish government is bringing into Cyprus primarily Anatolian peasants and shepherds, manual laborers, and smaller numbers of managers and retired military. The objectives of this colonization policy include:

- the systematic alteration of the demographic balance in Cyprus and the creation of a new political reality on the island;
- the alteration of the demographic balance of the Turkish Cypriot community;
- control of the political power and political developments in occupied Cyprus through voters dependent on the goodwill of the Turkish authorities;
- creation of de facto conditions prejudicing a future political settlement (humanitarian arguments, property allocation, power sharing ratios, etc.);
- provision of additional trained reserves to the occupation forces. The majority of the settlers are young men who have completed their military service in Turkey; and
- eradication of the Greek Cypriot cultural heritage and presence in the occupied areas.

Native Turkish Cypriot leaders lament the Turkish colonization of occupied Cyprus. Turkish Cypriot leaders like Mehmet Ali Talat (prior to becoming leader of the Turkish Cypriot community) and dissident political leaders like Ozger Ozgur, Mustafa Akinci, and many opposition newspaper editors have been critical of the manner by which citizenship has been granted to settlers, especially prior to elections in occupied Cyprus, questioned the preferential treatment given to settlers in the allocation of jobs and properties, and expressed concern over the cultural impact of settlers in an otherwise secular Muslim Turkish Cypriot community. The Cuco report on the settlers also points clearly to the tensions and conflicts created by the influx of settlers in a cohesive Turkish Cypriot community. Their impact has been felt in the outcome of elections and on the referendum on the Annan Plan, where the majority of the settlers voted in favor of the plan and provided the winning margin in the referendum in the occupied areas.[12] A settler political party and settler politicians have aligned themselves with the ruling coalition regime. Turkish Cypriot media report a notable increase in crime, money laundering, and the islamization of the occupied area. The islamization process has been enhanced by the inflow of Saudi Arabian money and the tolerant policies of civilian Turkish governments toward the revival of Islam. Settlers now constitute more than 90 percent of the population in the Karpass Peninsula and have become a major source of pressure and intimidation on the enclaved Greek Cypriots. Despite the criticism of the consequences of the Turkish colonization policy by Turkish Cypriot leaders, the process continues unabated. It is one more example of the inability of the Turkish Cypriot political leadership to stand up to the Turkish occupation authorities, and of the cooptation of leaders like Mehmet Ali Talat by the occupation authorities. His rise as a leader of the Turkish Cypriot community has muted his earlier criticism of Turkey's colonization policy.

The Illegality of the Colonization Policy and the International Response

Under international law, the transfer by an occupying power of its own civilian population into a territory it occupies is illegal. This is clearly stipulated in Article 46 (par. 6) of the Fourth Geneva Convention (1949) that Turkey has signed and ratified. Violation of this article constitutes a breach of this convention, opening the offending party to sanctions. This has not occurred because Turkey is supported by influential powers. In the Advisory Opinion of the International Court of Justice (2004), involving the construction by Israel of a wall in the occupied Palestinian territories, the court determined that any measures leading to the transfer of settlers to occupied territories are illegal. The 2004 protocol signed by Turkey and its subordinate local administration on the legalization of illegal Turkish nationals in the "TRNC" is an example of such a measure. Similar is the case of the provisions of Article 85 (par. 4a) of Protocol I of the 1949 Geneva Convention, and the provisions of Article 8 (par. 2b-viii) of the 1998 Rome Statute of the International Criminal Court.

Starting in 1978, the UN General Assembly in various resolutions[13] has deplored all unilateral actions to change the demographic structure of Cyprus. Similarly, the UN's Commission on Human Rights in various resolutions[14] called on the parties to refrain from changes to the demographic structure of Cyprus and expressed concern about the influx of settlers and the need to respect the rights and freedoms of the population of Cyprus. Resolutions by the UN Security Council and the General Assembly recognize and link the right of refugees and the displaced to return to their homes and properties to the presence of settlers.

The Turkish government continues to show its defiance of international law, and this has also been recognized by the Cuco and Laakso reports to the Parliamentary Assembly of the Council of Europe. In view of these developments, the Republic of Cyprus has proposed that:

- Turkey should introduce a moratorium on the influx of Turkish settlers in Cyprus;
- the Turkish government should adopt measures to facilitate the repatriation of Turkish settlers from Cyprus; and
- the Turkish government agree to an internationally supervised census on the size and composition of the population of occupied Cyprus, including the determination of persons entitled to citizenship under the terms of the 1960 Treaty of Establishment that created the independent Republic of Cyprus.

Cuco made a similar proposal in 1992. Turkey has shown no interest in either the request of the government of Cyprus or the suggestion by Cuco.

Conclusion

The deliberate and systematic Turkish colonization policy, following the ethnic cleansing that occurred in occupied Cyprus and the destruction of the Greek Cypriot cultural heritage, indicates Turkey's intentions in Cyprus. Turkey clearly aims at the creation of two ethnically cleansed states in Cyprus, hence its efforts to eradicate any evidence of Greek Cypriot presence or heritage in the area under its control. These measures, as documented by the Parliamentary Assembly of the Council of Europe, are not conducive to a mutually acceptable and peacefully negotiated solution to the Cyprus Problem, a solution that conforms to contemporary European and international law.

The Destruction of the Greek Cypriot Cultural Heritage

Turkey and its subordinate local administration have embarked on a systematic and deliberate policy to eradicate the Greek Cypriot cultural and historical heritage in the area under occupation. They have done so by:

- ethnic cleansing of the Greek Cypriot population, usurpation of their properties, and the refusal to allow the displaced and refugees to return to their homes and properties;

- the colonization of occupied Cyprus by Turkish Anatolian settlers who share none of the cultural characteristics of the island;
- the destruction of the Greek Cypriot cultural heritage in terms of religious monuments, artifacts, antiquities, and archaeological sites; and
- the systematic and deliberate change of names of towns, villages, and historical sites.

In a report to the Committee on Culture and Education of the Parliamentary Assembly of the Council of Europe,[15] General Rapporteur Van der Werff sought to identify how European support can be best assured for the protection of what is "an integral part of European cultural heritage."[16] After a visit to the occupied areas in 1976, British journalist J. Fielding wrote that "vandalism and desecration are so methodical and so widespread that they amount to institutionalized obliteration of everything sacred to a Greek."[17] Journalist Michael Jansen also noted that "the political-demographic partition imposed on Cyprus since 1974 thus threatens not only the unity and integrity of a modern nation-state but, also, the millennial cultural integrity and continuity of the island which has been the crossroads of the civilization of the eastern Mediterranean."[18]

Even Turkish Cypriots have been moved by the far-reaching effects of the destruction of Cypriot cultural heritage since the 1974 Turkish invasion. Turkish Cypriot journalist and poet Mehmet Yasin bemoaned how "Cyprus is being estranged from itself; the historic, environmental, cultural structure is being spoiled."[19] Similar assessments come from Turkish investigative journalist Ozgen Acar. They both point out how untended archaeological and religious sites are being pillaged and other sites destroyed by neglect and decay, while most sites have become objects of illegal exploitation by antique dealers with political connections to the authorities in occupied Cyprus.

The island of Cyprus as a whole is a major historical museum covering a chronological period of 11,000 years, from the Neolithic era to the present. Dr. Robin Cormack, expert consultant to the Committee on Culture and Education of the Parliamentary Assembly of the Council of Europe, has indicated that the cultural heritage of Cyprus is of central importance in the history of European art.[20] Reports by independent observers, European cultural institutions such "Europa Nostra," court testimonials, and other evidence presented in judicial proceedings all point to the fact that the systematic destruction of the Cypriot cultural heritage is one of the more tragic and irreversible consequences of the Turkish invasion and continuing occupation of northern Cyprus. This has happened despite international treaties signed and ratified by Turkey, including the 1954 UNESCO "Convention for the Protection of Cultural Property in the Event of Armed Conflict," the 1970 Convention "Prohibiting and Preventing the Illicit Import, Export and Transfer of Ownership of Cultural Property," and various protocols to the 1949 Geneva Conventions, among others.

As evidence of the destruction and looting of historical and religious sites and artifacts continued to mount and foreign journalists and UNESCO investigators reported on the situation, the Turkish Cypriot authorities adopted "law 35" on the protection of antiquities on 8 November 1975. Needless to say, this law has not been enforced. Two primary reasons account for this situation. One is the deliberate policy of eradicating all evidence of the Greek Cypriot cultural heritage, both historical and religious. The other is the huge amount of money involved in the smuggling and illegal sale of antiquities and religious artifacts on the international black market for stolen art objects. There are additional reasons for this. One is lack of knowledge and interest in the protection and restoration of religious art among Turkish Cypriots. Another is the unwillingness of the occupation authorities to commit the necessary resources for the protection and preservation of historic and religious sites and artifacts. This is a logical consequence of the decision to eradicate the Greek Cypriot cultural heritage. Finally, Turkish Cypriot authorities have attempted to use cooperation with agencies of the government of the Republic of Cyprus and other international agencies involved in the protection of cultural heritage. This attempt, however, was for political purposes, namely, for the de facto recognition of the "TRNC" and its government agencies.

Since the partial opening by the Turkish forces of the ceasefire line, the occupation authorities have encouraged visits by Greek Cypriot and other tourists to the occupied areas. This is why they opened to the public select historical and religious sites. For example, the Kyrenia ship, dating to 300 B.C., is on display in the medieval Kyrenia castle, much as it was prior to the Turkish invasion. The famous remains of the ship were nearly destroyed in 1976 due to the inability of the occupation authorities to maintain the required temperature and humidity in the display area.

Select churches have also been opened as "museums." Evidence of looting and destruction is evident in these churches.[21] Original icons, many dating to the tenth century and earlier, are missing and have been replaced by recent icons brought in from other nearby churches that are now closed, destroyed, or put to other uses. Other churches have had their Byzantine frescoes and mosaics whitewashed and/or plastered over, a practice dating back to the early days of the Ottoman conquest of Christian countries and territories.

Historical Importance

Situated at the crossroads of civilizations, Cyprus is a living cultural and historical museum with hundreds of archaeological sites dating from the Neolithic to the Greco-Roman period. It is a treasure house of medieval churches and religious art. Some 520 churches and 17 monasteries dot the landscape of occupied Cyprus. These churches and monasteries include notable Greek Orthodox and Maronite, Armenian, and Catholic sites.[22] The issue of the desecration, destruction, and looting of historic religious sites is of importance because of the close connection of religion and cultural heritage in Cyprus. A religious heritage dating back to the earliest days of Christianity is now at risk in occupied Cyprus. Cyprus is known to many as the "island of the saints," because some three hundred religious figures lived and were martyred on the island. Many of these sites that are important in Orthodox worship are located in the occupied areas and, until recently, were beyond the reach of the Greek Cypriot faithful. Moreover, every item in Orthodox, Maronite, and Armenian churches has a particular use and meaning to the faithful. These items (icons, vestments, religious implements, medieval manuscripts, etc.) have been looted, desecrated, or sold on the black market.

Investigations made possible especially since the 2003 partial opening of the ceasefire line documented fully the desecration of these religious sites. Seventy-eight (78) churches have been converted into mosques, twenty-eight (28) are used by the occupation forces as depots, dormitories, or hospitals, while thirteen (13) are used as stockyards, hay barns, etc. Others, like the church of St. Anastasia in Lapithos, have had their frescoes whitewashed, while the church edifice has been incorporated in a new luxury hotel/casino. Another historic church in Trimithi, in the Kyrenia region, is now used as an art school, while the famous medieval Armenian monastery of Sourp Magar, near the Pendadaktylos range, has been converted to a cafeteria because of its view and location. These are just few examples of what has happened to important religious sites in occupied Cyprus.

It should be noted that the fate of more than 15,000 portable religious icons, most of which date to the medieval period, is not known. We will return to this issue shortly. The same is the case involving thousands of ancient artifacts looted from museums, private collections, and excavation sites in occupied Cyprus. Many of these items have found their way to foreign buyers in the international black market and auction houses abroad. The recovery of these items will be discussed later in this section. Moreover, churches and archaeological sites have been destroyed for economic development reasons. Foreign archaeological schools excavated in Cyprus with the permission of the Department of Antiquities until 20 July 1974. The occupation authorities kicked them out, leaving important sites such as Salamis unprotected. Illegal excavations by local and Turkish groups continue, while the fate of archaeological finds is unknown. The occupation authorities have argued that the missing icons, religious artifacts, and antiquities have been gathered for "safekeeping" in select locations. However, they refuse any cooperation with the archaeological or ecclesiastical services of the Republic of Cyprus, while many historic and religious areas are off limits to visitors on the grounds that they are located in military districts.

Official Complicity

The involvement, at a high level, of the occupation authorities in the looting, desecration, destruction, removal, and illicit sale of important artifacts is well established. In the early post-invasion days, many of the artifacts were transported out of Cyprus on Turkish military trucks, naval vessels, and aircraft. Politics, the lure of money on the international black market for antiquities, and the intentional destruction of Cypriot cultural heritage will be illustrated by the following examples. Significant credit must be given to the work of journalist Michael Jansen, whose book *War and Cultural Heritage* minutely documents the intricate connections of international black marketeers and public authorities in the movement and illicit sale of Cypriot religious and archaeological artifacts.

On 14 September 1979, acting on a tip, the police in the Republic of Cyprus raided the home of UN Representative of the High Commissioner for Refugees Alfred zur Lippe-Weidenfeld. The police discovered in the home valuable antiquities and religious items from private collections and other sources that had been transported in UN vehicles with the assistance of members of UNFICYP. Even though Lippe-Weidenfeld was removed from Cyprus and eventually resigned from his UN post, no other action was taken against him because of the intervention on his behalf of former UN secretary-general Kurt Waldheim.

One of the first major investigations of the destruction of Cypriot cultural heritage was carried out in 1975 by a UNESCO envoy, Dalibard. He visited Cyprus on a two-month mission. Dalibard's detailed, one-hundred-page report not only pointed to the international significance of Cypriot cultural heritage but also recommended the establishment of a permanent UNESCO office in occupied Cyprus to supervise the protection of the various historic sites. Dalibard's major report was abbreviated to five pages, he himself was eventually removed from his position, and UNESCO was never able to open such an office in occupied Cyprus. Politics prevailed over the protection and preservation of historic sites.

The complicity of the occupation authorities in the removal and export of antiquities and religious items is best exemplified by the expert removal of frescoes and mosaics from walls of medieval Greek Orthodox churches. Without the required expertise, anyone attempting to remove frescoes and mosaics would destroy them. It is possible and probable that individuals carried out the theft of portable icons and other items. But the removal of mosaics and frescoes required scientific expertise, time, and technical support. Hence, local authorities had to be aware of these activities. Classic are the cases of the frescoes from the Church of Antiphonitis and the famous sixth-century mosaics from the Church of Kanakaria in Lythrangomi. The latter became the object of a major precedent-setting case in the United States.[23] The U.S. Circuit Court of Appeals for the Seventh Circuit affirmed the verdict of 3 August 1989 of the U.S. District Court in Indianapolis. The mosaics had been removed by Turkish antiquity smugglers and sold to an American art dealer for $1.2 million. The mosaics were returned to the Church of Cyprus and are now on display in the Byzantine Icons Museum in Nicosia. This precedent-setting U.S. federal court decision is important for the protection of cultural heritage in general.

Safeguarding the Cypriot Cultural Heritage

The recovery of stolen historical and religious artifacts is difficult for various reasons. One is the extensive black-market network in stolen art objects. These objects are often sold directly to private buyers worldwide. Such sales rarely see the light of day. Another complicating factor has been the absence of detailed church records, making difficult the proof of ownership in certain foreign jurisdictions. This painstaking process is slow, requires reliance on photographic and other evidence, and is often quite expensive. Private foundations and public and church funds have been used to buy back precious artifacts from international auction houses and other sources. On other occasions, compromises had to be made allowing temporary care and protection of such artifacts by foreign foundations.[24] In other instances, icons of lesser historical value in possession of foreign dealers have been traded for the return of more important ecclesiastical items. However, it ought to be mentioned that major museums, such as the British Museum and the Louvre, and major European auction houses have cooperated with the Republic of Cyprus to stop the sale and assist in the recovery and return of stolen Cypriot art.

The turkification of occupied Cyprus has taken another ominous turn since the early days following the invasion. That involves the deliberate and systematic change of the names of towns, villages, and other locations. This is part of the process of erasing the historical, cultural, and linguistic heritage of an area that can be traced back thousands of years. In addition to changing the cultural and demographic character of occupied Cyprus, the change in the geographic names is one more step in the process of eradicating the Greek Cypriot cultural heritage. Comparing maps published by the occupation authorities and by the Republic of Cyprus for the northern part of the island will illustrate this point. It is one more example of the Turkish government's disregard of international law.

The European Parliament has noted in repeated resolutions its concern over the destruction of the Cypriot cultural heritage and has called on Turkey and the Turkish Cypriots to entrust UNESCO with the preservation of the "Christian and Hellenic cultural heritage" of Cyprus.[25] Turkey has shown no sign of compliance. Sadly, UNESCO appears unable or unwilling to move on this issue, especially because the occupation authorities have sought de facto recognition by this UN agency in return for their cooperation.

The government of the Republic of Cyprus, along with the leadership of the Church of Cyprus, continues its efforts to not only rescue artifacts fundamental to the Cypriot cultural heritage but also inform the international community of the importance of collective action intended to protect the cultural heritage of victims of aggression and continuing occupation. With the partial opening of the ceasefire line, archaeologists have been able to travel to most areas outside military zones to informally assess the damage done to archaeological sites, religious sites, and museums. Dr. Ch. Chatzakoglou, a Greek Byzantinist, has recently compiled impressive evidence on the destruction of the Cypriot cultural heritage. The Kykkos Monastery has shared this evidence with appropriate government agencies. The purpose is to enhance efforts to promote the issue of the protection of the Cypriot cultural heritage at a time when Turkey is pursuing talks for accession to the EU.

The government of Cyprus has also undertaken bilateral agreements with other states intended to protect the Cypriot cultural heritage. Typical is the extension of the memorandum of understanding "To Protect the Archaeological and Ethnological Heritage of Cyprus" that was signed in Washington, D.C., on 20 July 2007. U.S. under-secretary of state Nicholas Burns stressed that this agreement was intended to help "preserve this incredible heritage that the Cypriot people enjoy and must protect." Ambassador Burns indicated that this agreement put "the full force of the American government and of our legal system . . . [to help] preserve these precious artifacts." The agreement covers Byzantine ecclesiastical and ritual ethnological materials and contains new restrictions on the import into the United States of pre-classical and classical archaeological objects from Cyprus.

In closing, the evidence presented speaks eloquently of the systematic and deliberate policies implemented in occupied Cyprus by the Turkish government and its agents, with the explicit purpose of eradicating the Greek Cypriot cultural heritage. Despite the international condemnation of Turkey's actions, these violations continue unabated. The implicit support extended to Turkey by external influential actors in the name of national security appears to assure Turkey of no sanctions for its documented and continuous violations of European and international law.

CHAPTER SEVEN

Cyprus and the European Human Rights Regime: Concluding Comments

THIS BOOK has not been written by a Cypriot, but by a friend of Cyprus who has visited both sides of this beautiful but divided island republic numerous times since 1976. It is a book written by an academic who has devoted much of his professional career to the rule of law, democracy, and human rights in American foreign policy. This book complements my earlier book, *Cyprus: A Contemporary Problem in Historical Perspective.* That volume examined the evolution of the Cyprus Problem over the last six decades and concluded with the prospects for a peaceful settlement based on the rules and principles of the European Union.

Because of the island's strategic location, considerations other than those of the rule of law, democracy, and human rights brought this British colony to independence in 1960. Strategic considerations of influential external parties also determined the evolution of the domestic problems that emerged in the implementation of the constitutional system that was imposed on the Cypriots as a precondition for independence. Even on the eve of the accession of the Republic of Cyprus to the European Union in the spring of 2004, the United States and Great Britain, working through the office of UN secretary-general Kofi Annan, attempted to impose a political settlement of the Cyprus problem that violated fundamental rules and principles of the European Union and the Council of Europe. In a free and fair referendum the Greek Cypriot public overwhelmingly rejected the 2004 Annan V arbitration plan. Had this plan been implemented, it would have made all Cypriots, Greek and Turkish, second-class EU citizens, deprived them of fundamental rights under the European Convention, and dissolved the internationally recognized Republic of Cyprus. The republic would have been replaced by a dysfunctional system based on the outcome of the Turkish invasion, the continuing occupation of Cyprus, and the continuing violations of human rights.

There is a domestic dimension to the Cyprus problem. The two Cypriot communities need to determine a power-sharing formula to replace the imposed system of the 1959 Zurich and London Agreements. Such a constitutional formula must be freely negotiated by the two communities and must be compatible with the principles of democracy, the rule of law, and human rights that are the foundation of the European Union and the Council of Europe.

This new formula must allow the Republic of Cyprus to meet its domestic, international, and EU obligations. No power-sharing formula will work if it violates the fundamentals of European law and the principles espoused by Article VI of the founding treaty of the EU. Resolution proposals based on ethnic separation, on the outcome of Turkey's 1974 invasion, and derogations from the EU standards of democracy, human rights, and the rule of law have no place in today's Europe.

The preceding chapters have shown that the Cyprus Problem today is the result of the 1974 Turkish invasion of the Republic of Cyprus, the continuing occupation of 37 percent of the territory of an EU member, and Turkey's documented and continuing violations of internationally recognized human rights. These violations of European law are not the product of Cypriot spin masters. Detailed and documented evidence of these violations have come from NGO investigations and from the conclusions of the European Commission of Human Rights in three Cypriot interstate applications by Cyprus against Turkey. Additional evidence has come from the decisions of the European Court of Human Rights in the fourth Cypriot interstate application against Turkey and rulings in the cases brought to the court by Greek Cypriots against Turkey. In addition, there are resolutions by the Parliamentary Assembly of the Council of Europe and the European Parliament, along with those of the UN Security Council and General Assembly, documenting Turkey's violations of European and international law.

The compliance by all members of the Council of Europe and the European Union with decisions of European legislative, semi-judicial, and judicial institutions shows that these institutions are seen as legitimate by their members. The only exception, according to the Parliamentary Assembly of the Council of Europe, is Turkey, even though it aspires to become a EU member.

The consistent thesis of this volume has been that the restoration of human rights in Cyprus will provide the foundation for the resolution of the Cyprus problem. The restoration of human rights cannot wait for a political settlement of the problem. It must be the foundation of a functional settlement that will conform to European law. This is why Cyprus remains a major testing ground of the primacy of democracy, the rule of law, and human rights in post-Cold War Europe, and of the emergent European human rights regime. Compromising on these principles in the name of political expediency will undermine the progress made in Europe over the last fifty years in the protection and promotion of human rights.

This volume examined in detail the emergence of a unique human rights regime in Europe in the aftermath of World War II, especially when compared to all other regions of the world. Turkey is a signatory of all major post- World War II European human rights treaties. Yet, it remains in violation of these treaties. This volume has provided grim details of the ethnic cleansing carried out against the Greek Cypriots because of their ethnicity, religion, and language. These documented and continuing violations show Turkey's total disregard of the European human rights regime. This was made possible in part by the support extended to Turkey, for strategic reasons, by influential members of the international community, support that has shielded that country from the threat of sanctions for its international misconduct. It is ironic that the guardian of international law, former UN secretary-general Kofi Annan, was willing to violate the European legal order in the name of political expediency with his proposed 2004 arbitration plan.

The evidence presented in this volume points clearly to Turkey's responsibility for the massive violations of human rights in Cyprus. Since 20 July 1974, Turkey remains in effective control of occupied Cyprus. This is why various court decisions also hold Turkey responsible for the acts of the Turkish Cypriot "subordinate local administration" in occupied Cyprus. Following its illegal invasion of Cyprus, Turkey proceeded with the ethnic cleansing of the occupied areas of the republic and has banned the return of Greek Cypriots to their homes and properties. It also implemented a massive demographic change and has proceeded with the destruction of the Greek Cypriot cultural heritage. These actions leave no doubt that Turkey's policies are deliberate, systematic, discriminatory, and aimed at Greek Cypriots because of their ethnicity, religion, and language. This is a flagrant violation of the European Convention of Human Rights and of Article VI of the founding treaty of the EU, an organization Turkey aspires to join.

Cyprus became a EU member in 2004, while Turkey is in accession talks with the EU. This presents an opportunity, for the first time in recent years, to bring about a settlement of the perpetuated Cyprus problem. A settlement based on the restoration of human rights, on European law, and on the principles of Article VI of the EU founding treaty will protect the rights of all Cypriots, Greek and Turkish alike.

Failure to take advantage of this opportunity will once again place *realpolitik* considerations above the rule of law, democracy, and human rights in post-Cold War Europe. This will undermine the progress made in Europe in the field of human rights over the last fifty years, will not contribute to stability in the Eastern Mediterranean, and will undermine the moral and legal stature, let alone the legitimacy, of European institutions. The challenge and the opportunity is in the hands of all well-meaning European interlocutors.

APPENDIX ONE

Resolutions on Cyprus by the European Parliament, the Parliamentary Assembly of the Council of Europe, and the Committee of Ministers of the Council of Europe

European Parliament

RESOLUTION 15 December 1988

condemning the destruction of cultural heritage in the Cypriot territory occupied by Turkey

The European Parliament,

A. having regard to its resolution on the situation in Cyprus of 20 May 1988 (COSTE-FLORET report, Doc. A 2-317/87),
B. stressing how important it is for the peoples of Europe and European culture that the Christian and Hellenic culture which has developed in Cyprus over 9000 years be protected and safeguarded,
C. deeply concerned at the continued destruction and pillaging of the Christian and Hellenic cultural heritage in the occupied territories in Cyprus,

1. Condemns the continued destruction and pillaging of the Christian and Hellenic cultural heritage in the occupied territories;
2. Calls on the Council of Ministers, pursuant to paragraph 10 of the European Parliament's resolution to take appropriate measures immediately to ensure that the Turkish authorities and the representatives of the Turkish Cypriot community agree to entrust to UNESCO the task of protecting the Christian and Hellenic cultural heritage in the occupied part of the island;
3. Considers that, if Turkey wishes to strengthen its ties with the European Communities, it should, inter alia, in keeping with the conventions and principles of international law, respect what is a profoundly European cultural heritage;
4. Instructs its President to forward this written declaration to the Council of Ministers, the governments of Turkey and Cyprus and UNESCO.

RESOLUTION 12 September 1991

on the lack of Community involvement in resolving the Cyprus question

The European Parliament,

A. having regard to the urgent need for a 'just and lasting' solution to the Cyprus problem involving the full implementation of the UN's decisions,
B. having regard also to the European Community's keen interest in restoring international legitimacy and guaranteeing peace, normality and stability in the Eastern Mediterranean,
C. whereas the continued Turkish military occupation of more than 35% of the territory of Cyprus and the systematic attempt at colonisation have created, inter alia, approximately 200 000 refugees while the fate of some 2 000 Greek Cypriots is still unknown and whereas this serious abnormal international situation is affecting the independent Republic of Cyprus which is associated with the European Community,
D. noting the repeated decisions of the UN and the resolutions of the European Parliament concerning the planned international conference in which the USA and the Soviet Union are seeking to take part,

1. Considers that the lack of involvement of the European Community in finding a solution to the Cyprus question is incomprehensible;
2. Calls on the European Council and the Council of Ministers to take the necessary steps to ensure that the European Community takes part in the conference which is of major importance for the whole of Europe;
3. Instructs its President to forward this resolution to the Council and Commission.

RESOLUTION 27 March 1996

The European Parliament,

—having regard to its previous resolutions on the situation in Cyprus,

A. whereas the next enlargement of the European Union will include Cyprus, according to the conclusions of the recent European Councils,
B. whereas accession negotiations with Cyprus will start six months after the end of the 1996 Intergovernmental Conference, as provided for in the 6 March 1995 decision,
C. having regard to the progress made during the structured dialogue and the progress made by Cyprus in adapting to the acquis communautaire,
D. having regard to the need for a just and viable solution to the Cyprus problem based on international law and the relevant United Nations resolutions and in conformity with Community norms,
E. having regard to recent statements by Mr Denktash, according to which the 1619 Greek Cypriots whose fate has been unknown since 1974 were arrested

and handed over by the Turkish army to Turkish Cypriot paramilitary organisations and were killed by them; considering that the responsibility for their fate lies with Turkey, according to the 1949 Geneva Conventions and their Protocols, the 1907 Regulation of the Hague and international customary law,

F. having regard to the refusal of the occupation regime to allow a mission of the Sub-committee on Human Rights of the European Parliament to visit the Greek Cypriot enclave in the occupied part of Cyprus,
G. having regard to the continuing and systematic destruction of the cultural heritage of the occupied part of Cyprus,
H. having regard to the decision of the Italian Presidency to appoint a representative for the Cyprus problem as well as the fact that the structured dialogue has already begun and shows positive progress,

1. Condemns the content of recent statements by Mr Denktash on the killing of the 1619 Greek Cypriots and demands that the European Union do everything in its power so that the fate of the missing persons will be cleared up;
2. Demands that Turkey cooperate in honesty and good faith in ascertaining the fate of all missing persons by providing the necessary information for each one of them to the United Nations Committee for Missing Persons;
3. Condemns the refusal of the occupation regime to allow a delegation from the European Parliament to visit the Greek Cypriot enclave, a fact constituting an affront to the Parliament itself;
4. Demands that Turkey take all necessary measures so that the delegation from the European Parliament visit the enclave in order to examine the living conditions and submit a relevant report for consideration, in the first instance, by the European Parliament's Sub-committee on Human Rights;
5. Asks the Turkish side to put an end to the destruction of the cultural heritage of the occupied part of Cyprus and allow the Cyprus Archeological Department, as well as foreign archeological teams, to visit the archeological sites and churches in the occupied part of Cyprus;
6. Welcomes the initiative by the Italian Presidency to appoint a representative for the Cyprus problem and asks the Council to upgrade this initiative through joint action and a common initiative with a view to solving the Cyprus problem in accordance with paragraph 19 of the European Parliament's resolution of 12 July 1995 on Cyprus's application for membership of the European Union; asks however for this role to be clearly defined, and for it to be made clear whether the representative will express proposals and/or recommendations, the contents of which must in any case be communicated to the European Parliament;
7. Welcomes the proposal of the Cyprus government for the demilitarisation of Cyprus and asks Turkey to withdraw its occupation forces from the island and abide by the United Nations resolutions on Cyprus;
8. Instructs its President to forward this resolution to the Commission, the Council, the governments and parliaments of Cyprus and Turkey and the UN.

RESOLUTION 15 November 2000 (Extracts)

on Turkey's progress towards accession

European Parliament resolution on the 1999 Regular Report
from the Commission on Turkey's progress towards accession
(COM(1999) 513 - C5-0036/2000 - 2000/2014(COS))
The European Parliament,

J. whereas Resolution 1250 of the UN Security Council called on the Turkish
and Greek Cypriot communities to begin negotiations in the autumn of 1999,
and whereas no progress in that direction has been recorded, despite the encouraging contacts made under the aegis of the UN Secretary-General in December 1999 and in January 2000; regretting, on the contrary, the violation of
the military status quo by Turkish occupation forces in the village of Strovilia
since 1 July 2000,
K. whereas the judgment of the European Court of Human Rights in 'Loïzidou
v Turkey' (No 15318/89), handed down on 28 July 1998 and ruling in favour of
the plaintiff, has still not been implemented,

18. Calls on the Turkish Government, in accordance with Resolution 1250 of
the UN Security Council, to contribute towards the creation, without precondi-
tions, of a climate conducive to negotiations between the Greek and Turkish
Cypriot communities, with a view to reaching a negotiated, comprehensive,
just and lasting settlement which complies with the relevant UN Security
Council resolutions and the recommendations of the UN General Assembly, as
reaffirmed by the European Council; hopes that this will be possible during the
fifth round of proximity talks which will begin on 10 November 2000 and that
those talks will result in bilateral negotiations, under the aegis of the UN,
which will enable substantial progress to be made;
19. Calls on the Turkish Government to withdraw its occupation forces from
northern Cyprus;

24. Calls on the Turkish Government to comply with previous and future decisions of the European Court of Human Rights...

Parliamentary Assembly of the Council of Europe

RECOMMENDATION 1197 (1992) 7 October 1992

on the demographic structure of the Cypriot communities

1. Historic events led to the de facto division of the island of Cyprus into two
parts. Almost the entire Greek Cypriot community lives in the southern part,
controlled by the Government of the Republic of Cyprus. Almost the entire

Turkish Cypriot community lives in the northern part controlled by the Turkish Cypriot administration.

2. According to the Government of the Republic of Cyprus, the population in the southern part was estimated at 575 000 at the end of 1990, whereas the figure was 505 700 for 1974. This would give a rate of increase of 13,7% for the period 1974 to 1990.

3. According to the Turkish Cypriot administration, the population in the northern part was estimated to be 171 500 at the end of 1990, as against 115 600 in 1974. This would give a rate of increase of 48,35% for the period 1974-90.

4. As the natural rates of increase in the population, based on the number of births and deaths, are comparable in both parts of the island, the population growth in the north must be due to a substantial influx of migrants.

5. It is an established fact that, from 1975 onwards, Turkish nationals arrived in the northern part of Cyprus, where they settled on a long-term basis. The waves of migrants were particularly large in 1975 and 1977 because, even on the lowest estimates, they represented 10% of the Turkish Cypriot population at that time. Subsequently, there was a smaller, but steady flow. A fairly visible presence of Turkish armed forces is also to be noted in the northern part of the island.

6. The aim of the Turkish Cypriot administration's policy regarding the Turkish migrants has been to encourage their permanent settlement in the island. Migrants are granted housing, land or properties on special terms. However, the most important measure has been to allow them to acquire Cypriot nationality and hence political rights. The legal texts give the authorities discretionary power in this matter.

7. The Greek Cypriots are extremely concerned at the arrival of the Turkish migrants. At first, the Turkish Cypriots regarded this injection of manpower as essential. Today, the growing number of migrants, their naturalisation and the important role that some of them play in political life have given rise to wide divergences within the Turkish Cypriot community.

8. The presence and naturalisation of the Turkish migrants, who once established on the island become settlers, constitute an additional obstacle to a peaceful, negotiated solution of the Cypriot conflict.

9. The Assembly therefore recommends that the Committee of Ministers:

i. instruct the European Population Committee (CDPO) to conduct a census of the island's population, in co-operation with the authorities concerned, in order to replace population estimates with reliable data;

ii. request the authorities of the Republic of Cyprus and the Turkish Cypriot administration to keep the arrival of aliens on the island under strict control;

iii. appeal to the Turkish Cypriot administration to reconsider the legislation on naturalisation in force in the part of the island it controls, so that no changes in the demographic structure of the island result from the application of such legislation;

iv. promote the establishment of a climate of trust between the two Cypriot communities;

v. invite the guarantor powers of the Republic of Cyprus to respect the provisions of the 1959 agreements scrupulously, especially with regard to the presence of armed forces in the island;

vi. invite Turkey to register in its Cyprus consulate all Turkish citizens residing and arriving in Cyprus;

vii. give its full support to the efforts of the Secretary-General of the United Nations to achieve the rapid re-establishment in the whole of Cyprus of a law-based state accepted by both communities.

RECOMMENDATION 1546 (2002) 22 January (2002)

on the implementation of decisions of the European Court of Human Rights

1. The Assembly refers to its Resolution 1268 (2002) on the implementation of decisions of the European Court of Human Rights.

2. It refers also to its Resolution 1226 (2000) and Recommendation 1477 (2000) on the execution of judgments of the European Court of Human Rights, in which it asked the Committee of Ministers to take a number of measures to facilitate the implementation of the Court's judgments.

3. It regrets that, one year later, the Committee of Ministers has still not replied to the recommendation.

4. The Assembly accordingly reiterates its recommendations to the Committee of Ministers:

i. to amend the European Convention on Human Rights so as to give the Committee of Ministers the power to ask the Court for a clarifying interpretation of its judgments where necessary, and to introduce a system of astreintes (daily fines for delays in the performance of a legal obligation) to be imposed on states that persistently fail to execute a Court judgment;

ii. to ask the governments of High Contracting Parties to make more use of their right to intervene in cases before the Court;

iii. to be more firm in carrying out its functions under Article 46 of the Convention;

iv. to ensure that measures taken by governments constitute effective means to prevent further violations being committed.

5. The Assembly welcomes the report of the Evaluation Group of the Committee of Ministers on the European Court of Human Rights.

6. It also recommends that a wider range of responses be developed to cases of failure of Member States to abide by the human rights standards of the Council of Europe, bearing in mind existing proposals.

7. In this context, the Parliamentary Assembly also strongly supports the Committee of Ministers' appeal to the authorities of the Member States to take whatever action they deem necessary to ensure the proper execution of judgments in situations where the Committee of Ministers has found the respondent state to be in breach of its fundamental obligation under the Convention

to comply with the judgments of the European Court of Human Rights as it did in the Loizidou case (see Interim Resolution Res DH(2001)80).

RECOMMENDATION 1608 (2003) 24 June 2003

on the colonisation by Turkish settlers of the occupied part of Cyprus

1. The Parliamentary Assembly expresses its deep disappointment at the failure of the negotiations under the aegis of the United Nations aimed at achieving a functional and viable solution to the Cyprus problem. It hopes, nevertheless, that the efforts will be resumed and continued until a sustainable settlement is found.
2. It is a well-established fact that the demographic structure of the island has been continuously modified since its de facto partition in 1974, as a result of the deliberate policies of the Turkish Cypriot administration and Turkey. Despite the lack of consensus on the exact figures, all parties concerned admit that Turkish nationals have since been systematically arriving in the northern part of the island. According to reliable estimates, their number currently totals 115 000.
3. The settlers come mainly from the region of Anatolia, one of the least developed regions of Turkey. Their customs and traditions differ significantly from those present in Cyprus. These differences are the main cause of the tensions and dissatisfaction of the indigenous Turkish Cypriot population, who tend to view the settlers as a foreign element.
4. In particular, the Assembly expresses its concern at the continuous outflow of the indigenous Turkish Cypriot population from the northern part of the island. Their number decreased from 118 000 in 1974 to an estimated 87 600 in 2001. In consequence, the settlers outnumber the indigenous Turkish Cypriot population in the northern part.
5. In the light of the information available, the Assembly cannot accept the claims that the majority of arriving Turkish nationals are seasonal workers or former inhabitants who had left the island before 1974. Therefore it condemns the policy of "naturalisation" designed to encourage new arrivals which was introduced by the Turkish Cypriot administration with the full support of the Government of Turkey.
6. The Assembly is convinced that the presence of the settlers constitutes a process of hidden colonisation and an additional and important obstacle to a peaceful negotiated solution of the Cyprus problem.
7. Therefore, the Assembly recommends that the Committee of Ministers:

i. instruct the European Population Committee (CAHP) to conduct a population census of the whole island, in co-operation with the authorities concerned, in order to replace estimates with reliable data;
ii. promote the idea of the creation, with a contribution from the international community, of a fund which would ensure the financing of any voluntary returns of the Turkish settlers to Turkey;

iii. encourage the involvement of the Council of Europe Development Bank and call on the governments of Turkey and Cyprus to present concrete return projects for financing;

iv. call on Turkey, as well as its Turkish Cypriot subordinate local administration in northern Cyprus, to stop the process of colonisation by Turkish settlers and, in particular, call on the Turkish Cypriot administration to review their migration legislation and policies, and especially the law on naturalisation, with a view to revising them and, in consequence, bringing them into line with international standards;

v. call on Turkey to comply with the decisions of the European Court of Human Rights concerning refugees' right to property in the occupied part of Cyprus;

vi. promote contacts and dialogue between the civil societies of the Greek Cypriot and Turkish Cypriot communities.

RESOLUTION 1333 (2003) 24 June 2003

on the rights and fundamental freedoms of Greek Cypriots and Maronites living in the northern part of Cyprus

1. The Parliamentary Assembly once again expresses its serious concern that the island of Cyprus continues to be rigorously and arbitrarily divided into two parts and that this situation has lasted for over thirty years without any improvement.

2. All the people living in Cyprus, in the northern as well as the southern part, have been protected by the European Convention on Human Rights since the Republic of Cyprus acceded to this Convention on 6 October 1962.

3. The Assembly agrees with the opinion expressed by the European Court of Human Rights, clearly stated in its judgment of 10 May 2001 in the case of Cyprus v. Turkey, that Turkey's responsibility under the Convention also extends to acts of the Turkish Cypriot administration: Turkey therefore has a general obligation to secure respect for the human rights safeguarded by the Convention for all persons within the territory controlled by the Turkish Cypriot administration.

4. The Assembly is extremely concerned by the status imposed upon the Greek Cypriot and Maronite communities that have remained north of the demarcation line and by the resulting violations of human rights, as established by the European Court of Human Rights in Strasbourg.

5. The Assembly none the less welcomes the recent positive developments in Cyprus, especially the opening of borders and granting of freedom of movement, which could considerably improve the situation of the Greek Cypriots and Maronites who have remained north of the demarcation line.

6. The Assembly considers that a general settlement of the Cypriot conflict should never be achieved at the expense of the communities that have chosen to stay where they have always resided.

7. The Assembly acknowledges and agrees with the conclusions of the above-mentioned Cyprus v. Turkey judgment, in which the European Court of Hu-

man Rights established that there had been violations of the human rights of the Greek Cypriot and Maronite communities living in the northern part of Cyprus.

8. The Assembly is particularly shocked by the imposed division of families, the prohibition on young people returning to their homes, the arbitrary confiscations and expropriations and the general climate of apprehension and uncertainty, even fear, to which members of these communities are deliberately subjected.

9. The Assembly insists that the Turkish Cypriot administration controlling the northern part of Cyprus, as well as Turkey, which assumes de facto legal co-responsibility in this part of the island as indicated in paragraph 3 above:

i. cease all humiliation of the Greek and Maronite communities and put an end to the climate of intimidation;

ii. end the dispossessions affecting members of these communities by returning to them the property and possessions of which they have been arbitrarily dispossessed, individually or collectively, or failing that offer them just compensation;

iii. ensure freedom of education and worship for Orthodox Christians and Maronites;

iv. end all the restrictions on movements across the demarcation line and immediately grant Greek Cypriots living in the northern part of Cyprus at least the same rights as those already granted to Maronites;

v. grant all inhabitants the right to an effective remedy;

vi. ensure equal access to medical care;

vii. permit the communities to freely choose their own representatives.

10. The Assembly urges all the representatives of the civil society of Cyprus, regardless of the community to which they belong, to do their utmost to bring about a climate of mutual understanding, of dialogue and of tolerance between the different social, political, religious, cultural and linguistic constituents present on the island, whose history shows that they are perfectly capable of living together in peace and harmony.

Council of Europe Committee of Ministers

INTERIM RESOLUTION DH (2001) 80

concerning the judgment of the European Court of Human Rights of 28 July 1998 in the case of Loizidou against Turkey

(Adopted by the Committee of Ministers on 26 June 2001 at the 757th meeting of the Ministers' Deputies)

The Committee of Ministers, acting under the terms of former Article 54 of the Convention for the Protection of Human Rights and Fundamental Freedoms ("the Convention" below),

Having regard to the judgment of the European Court of Human Rights ("the Court" below) of 28 July 1998 which ordered Turkey to pay to the applicant before 28 October 1998 specific sums for damages and for costs and expenses;

Recalling its Interim Resolution DH (2000) 105, in which it declared that the refusal of Turkey to execute the judgment of the Court demonstrated a manifest disregard for Turkey's international obligations, both as a High Contracting Party to the Convention and as a Member State of the Council of Europe, and strongly insisted that, in view of the gravity of the matter, Turkey comply fully and without any further delay with this judgment;

Very deeply deploring the fact that, to date, Turkey has still not complied with its obligations under this judgment;

Stressing that every Member State of the Council of Europe must accept the principles of the rule of law and of the enjoyment by all persons within its jurisdiction of human rights and fundamental freedoms;
Stressing that acceptance of the Convention, including the compulsory jurisdiction of the Court and the binding nature of its judgments, has become a requirement for membership of the organisation;

Stressing that the Convention is a system for the collective enforcement of the rights protected therein;

Declares the Committee's resolve to ensure, with all means available to the organisation Turkey's compliance with its obligations under this judgment;

Calls upon the authorities of the Member States to take such action as they deem appropriate to this end.

APPENDIX TWO

United Nations Resolutions on Cyprus

Security Council

Resolution 186 (1964)
4 March 1964

The Security Council,
Noting that the present situation with regard to Cyprus is likely to threaten international peace and security and may further deteriorate unless additional measures are promptly taken to maintain peace and to seek out a durable solution,
Considering the positions taken by the parties in relation to the Treaties signed at Nicosia on 16 August 1960,
Having in mind the relevant provisions of the Charter of the United Nations and, in particular, its Article 2, paragraph 4, which reads:
"All Members shall refrain in their international relations from the threat or use of force against the territorial integrity or political independence of any State, or in any other manner inconsistent with the purposes of the United Nations",
1. *Calls upon* all Member States, in conformity with their obligations under the Charter of the United Nations, to refrain from any action or threat of action likely to worsen the situation in the sovereign Republic of Cyprus, or to endanger international peace;
2. *Asks* the Government of Cyprus, which has the responsibility for the maintenance and restoration of law and order, to take all additional measures necessary to stop violence and bloodshed in Cyprus;
3. *Calls upon* the communities in Cyprus and their leaders to act with the utmost restraint;
4. *Recommends* the creation, with the consent of the Government of Cyprus, of a United Nations Peace-keeping Force in Cyprus. The composition and size of the Force shall be established by the Secretary-General, in consultation with the Governments of Cyprus, Greece, Turkey and the United Kingdom of Great Britain and Northern Ireland. The Commander of the Force shall be appointed by the Secretary-General and report to him. The Secretary-General,

who shall keep the Governments providing the Force fully informed, shall report periodically to the Security Council on its operation;

5. *Recommends* that the function of the Force should be, in the interest of preserving international peace and security, to use its best efforts to prevent a recurrence of fighting and, as necessary, to contribute to the maintenance and restoration of law and order and a return to normal conditions;

6. *Recommends* that the stationing of the Force shall be for a period of three months, all costs pertaining to it being met, in a manner to be agreed upon by them, by the Governments providing the contingents and by the Government of Cyprus. The Secretary-General may also accept voluntary contributions for that purpose;

7. *Recommends further* that the Secretary-General designate, in agreement with the Government of Cyprus and the Governments of Greece, Turkey and the United Kingdom, a mediator, who shall use his best endeavours with the representatives of the communities and also with the aforesaid four Governments, for the purpose of promoting a peaceful solution and an agreed settlement of the problem confronting Cyprus, in accordance with the Charter of the United Nations, having in mind the well-being of the people of Cyprus as a whole and the preservation of international peace and security. The mediator shall report periodically to the Secretary-General on his efforts;

8. *Requests* the Secretary-General to provide, from funds of the United Nations, as appropriate, for the remuneration and expenses of the mediator and his staff.

Adopted unanimously at the 1102nd meeting.

Resolution 353 (1974)
20 July 1974

The Security Council,
Having considered the report of the Secretary-General, at its 1779th meeting, about the recent developments in Cyprus,
Having heard the statement of the President of the Republic of Cyprus and the statements of the representatives of Cyprus, Turkey, Greece and other Member States,
Having considered at its present meeting further developments in the island,
Deeply deploring the outbreak of violence and the continuing bloodshed,
Gravely concerned about the situation which has led to a serious threat to international peace and security, and which has created a most explosive situation in the whole Eastern Mediterranean area,
Equally concerned about the necessity to restore the constitutional structure of the Republic of Cyprus, established and guaranteed by international agreements,
Recalling its resolution 186 (1964) of 4 March 1964 and its subsequent resolutions on this matter,

Conscious of its primary responsibility for the maintenance of international peace and security in accordance with Article 24 of the Charter of the United Nations,

1. *Calls upon* all States to respect the sovereignty, independence and territorial integrity of Cyprus;

2. *Calls upon* all parties to the present fighting as a first step to cease all firing and requests all States to exercise the utmost restraint and to refrain from any action which might further aggravate the situation;

3. *Demands* an immediate end to foreign military intervention in the Republic of Cyprus that is in contravention of the provisions of paragraph 1 above;

4. *Requests* the withdrawal without delay from the Republic of Cyprus of foreign military personnel present otherwise than under the authority of international agreements, including those whose withdrawal was requested by the President of the Republic of Cyprus, Archbishop Makarios, in his letter of 2 July 1974;

5. *Calls upon* Greece, Turkey and the United Kingdom of Great Britain and Northern Ireland to enter into negotiations without delay for the restoration of peace in the area and constitutional government in Cyprus and to keep the Secretary-General informed;

6. *Calls upon* all parties to co-operate fully with the United Nations Peace-keeping Force in Cyprus to enable it to carry out its mandate;

7. *Decides* to keep the situation under constant review and asks the Secretary-General to report as appropriate with a view to adopting further measures in order to ensure that peaceful conditions are restored as soon as possible.

Adopted unanimously at the 1781st meeting.

Resolution 360 (1974)
16 August 1974

The Security Council,
Recalling its resolutions 353 (1974) of 20 July, 354 (1974) of 23 July, 355 (1974) of 1 August, 357 (1974) of 14 August and 358 (1974) of 15 August 1974,
Noting that all States have declared their respect for the sovereignty, independence and territorial integrity of the Republic of Cyprus,
Gravely concerned at the deterioration of the situation in Cyprus, resulting from the further military operations, which constituted a most serious threat to peace and security in the Eastern Mediterranean area,

1. *Records its formal disapproval* of the unilateral military actions undertaken against the Republic of Cyprus;

2. *Urges* the parties to comply with all the provisions of previous resolutions of the Security Council, including those concerning the withdrawal without delay from the Republic of Cyprus of foreign military personnel present otherwise than under the authority of international agreements;

3. *Urges* the parties to resume without delay, in an atmosphere of constructive co-operation, the negotiations called for in resolution 353 (1974) whose

outcome should not be impeded or prejudged by the acquisition of advantages resulting from military operations;

4. *Requests* the Secretary-General to report to the Council, as necessary, with a view to the possible adoption of further measures designed to promote the restoration of peaceful conditions;

5. *Decides* to remain seized of the question permanently and to meet at any time to consider measures which may be required in the light of the developing situation.

> *Adopted at the 1794th meeting by 11 votes to none with 3 abstentions (Byelorussian Soviet Socialist Republic, Iraq, Union of Soviet Socialist Republics).*

Resolution 361 (1974)
30 August 1974

The Security Council,
Conscious of its special responsibilities under the United Nations Charter,
Recalling its resolutions 186 (1964) of 4 March 1964, 353 (1974) of 20 July, 354 (1974) of 23 July, 355 (1974) of 1 August, 357 (1974) of 14 August, 358 (1974) and 359 (1974) of 15 August and 360 (1974) of 16 August 1974,
Noting that a large number of people in Cyprus have been displaced, and are in dire need of humanitarian assistance,
Mindful of the fact that it is one of the foremost purposes of the United Nations to lend humanitarian assistance in situations such as the one currently prevailing in Cyprus,
Noting also that the United Nations High Commissioner for Refugees has already been appointed Co-ordinator of United Nations Humanitarian Assistance for Cyprus, with the task of co-ordinating relief assistance to be provided by United Nations programmes and agencies and from other sources,
Having considered the report of the Secretary-General contained in document S/11473,

1. *Expresses its appreciation* to the Secretary-General for the part he has played in bringing about talks between the leaders of the two communities in Cyprus;

2. *Warmly welcomes* this development and calls upon those concerned in the talks to pursue them actively with the help of the Secretary-General and in the interests of the Cypriot people as a whole;

3. *Calls upon* all parties to do everything in their power to alleviate human suffering, to ensure the respect of fundamental human rights for every person and to refrain from all action likely to aggravate the situation;

4. *Expresses its grave concern* at the plight of the refugees and other persons displaced as a result of the situation in Cyprus and urges the parties concerned, in conjunction with the Secretary-General, to search for peaceful solutions to the problems of refugees and take appropriate measures to provide for their relief and welfare and to permit persons who wish to do so to return to their homes in safety;

5. *Requests* the Secretary-General to submit at the earliest possible opportunity a full report on the situation of the refugees and other persons referred to in paragraph 4 above and decides to keep that situation under constant review;

6. *Further requests* the Secretary-General to continue to provide emergency United Nations humanitarian assistance to all parts of the population of the island in need of such assistance;

7. *Calls upon* all parties, as a demonstration of good faith, to take, both individually and in co-operation with each other, all steps which may promote comprehensive and successful negotiations;

8. *Reiterates* its call to all parties to co-operate fully with the United Nations Peace-keeping Force in Cyprus in carrying out its tasks;

9. *Expresses the conviction* that the speedy implementation of the provisions of the present resolution will assist the achievement of a satisfactory settlement in Cyprus.

Adopted unanimously at the 1795th meeting.

Resolution 541 (1983)
18 November 1983

The Security Council,
Having heard the statement of the Foreign Minister of the Government of the Republic of Cyprus,

Concerned at the declaration by the Turkish Cypriot authorities issued on 15 November 1983 which purports to create an independent state in northern Cyprus,

Considering that this declaration is incompatible with the 1960 Treaty concerning the establishment of the Republic of Cyprus and the 1960 Treaty of Guarantee,

Considering, therefore, that the attempt to create a "Turkish Republic of Northern Cyprus" is invalid, and will contribute to a worsening of the situation in Cyprus,

Reaffirming its resolutions 365 (1974) and 367 (1975),

Aware of the need for a solution of the Cyprus problem based on the mission of good offices undertaken by the Secretary-General,

Affirming its continuing support for the United Nations Peace-keeping Force in Cyprus,

Taking note of the Secretary-General's statement of 17 November 1983,

1. *Deplores* the declaration of the Turkish Cypriot authorities of the purported secession of part of the Republic of Cyprus;

2. *Considers* the declaration referred to above as legally invalid and calls for its withdrawal;

3. *Calls for* the urgent and effective implementation of its resolutions 365 (1974) and 367 (1975);

4. *Requests* the Secretary-General to pursue his mission of good offices, in order to achieve the earliest possible progress towards a just and lasting settlement in Cyprus;

5. *Calls upon* the parties to co-operate fully with the Secretary-General in his mission of good offices;

6. *Calls upon* all States to respect the sovereignty, independence, territorial integrity and non-alignment of the Republic of Cyprus;

7. *Calls upon* all States not to recognise any Cypriot State other than the Republic of Cyprus;

8. *Calls upon* all States and the two communities in Cyprus to refrain from any action which might exacerbate the situation;

9. *Requests* the Secretary-General to keep the Security Council fully informed.

Adopted at the 2500th meeting by 13 votes to 1 against (Pakistan),
with 1 abstention (Jordan).

Resolution 550 (1984)
11 May 1984

The Security Council,

Having considered the situation in Cyprus at the request of the Government of the Republic of Cyprus,

Having heard the statement made by the President of the Republic of Cyprus,

Taking note of the report of the Secretary-General,

Recalling its resolutions 365 (1974), 367 (1975), 541 (1983) and 544 (1983),

Deeply regretting the non-implementation of its resolutions, in particular resolution 541 (1983),

Gravely concerned about the further secessionist acts in the occupied part of the Republic of Cyprus which are in violation of resolution 541 (1983), namely, the purported exchange of ambassadors between Turkey and the legally invalid "Turkish Republic of Northern Cyprus" and the contemplated holding of a "constitutional referendum" and "elections", as well as by other actions or threats of actions aimed at further consolidating the purported independent State and the division of Cyprus,

Deeply concerned about recent threats for settlement of Varosha by people other than its inhabitants,

Reaffirming its continuing support for the United Nations Peace-keeping Force in Cyprus,

1. *Reaffirms* its resolution 541 (1983) and calls for its urgent and effective implementation;

2. *Condemns* all secessionist actions, including the purported exchange of ambassadors between Turkey and the Turkish Cypriot leadership, declares them illegal and invalid and calls for their immediate withdrawal;

3. *Reiterates* the call upon all States not to recognize the purported State of the "Turkish Republic of Northern Cyprus" set up by secessionist acts and calls upon them not to facilitate or in any way assist the aforesaid secessionist entity;

4. *Calls upon* all States to respect the sovereignty, independence, territorial integrity, unity and non-alignment of the Republic of Cyprus;

5. *Considers* attempts to settle any part of Varosha by people other than its inhabitants as inadmissible and calls for the transfer of that area to the administration of the United Nations;

6. *Considers* any attempts to interfere with the status or the deployment of the United Nations Peace-keeping Force in Cyprus as contrary to the resolutions of the United Nations;

7. *Requests* the Secretary-General to promote the urgent implementation of Security Council resolution 541 (1983);

8. *Reaffirms* the mandate of good offices given to the Secretary-General and requests him to undertake new efforts to attain an overall solution to the Cyprus problem in conformity with the principles of the Charter of the United Nations and the provisions for such a settlement laid down in the pertinent United Nations resolutions, including resolution 541 (1983) and the present resolution;

9. *Calls upon* all parties to co-operate with the Secretary-General in his mission of good offices;

10. *Decides* to remain seized of the situation with a view to taking urgent and appropriate measures, in the event of non-implementation of resolution 541 (1983) and the present resolution;

11. *Requests* the Secretary-General to promote the implementation of the present resolution and to report thereon to the Security Council as developments require.

Adopted at the 2539th meeting by 13 votes to 1 (Pakistan), with 1 abstention (United States of America).

General Assembly

3450 (XXX)
Missing persons in Cyprus

The General Assembly,
Recalling its resolution 3212 (XXIX) of 1 November 1974,
Noting resolution 4 (XXXI) adopted by the Commission on Human Rights on 13 February 1975,
Gravely concerned about the fate of a considerable number of Cypriots who are missing as a result of armed conflict in Cyprus,
Appreciating the work of the International Committee of the Red Cross in this field,
Reaffirming the basic human need of families in Cyprus to be informed about missing relatives,

1. *Requests* the Secretary-General to exert every effort, in close co-operation with the International Committee of the Red Cross, to assist in tracing and accounting for persons missing as a result of armed conflict in Cyprus;

2. *Requests* the Secretary-General to provide the Commission on Human Rights at its thirty-second session with information relevant to the implementation of the present resolution.

2433rd plenary meeting
9 December 1975

[Adopted by 106 votes to none with 26 abstentions]

37/253 (1983)
Question of Cyprus

The General Assembly,
Having considered the question of Cyprus,
Recalling its resolution 3212 (XXIX) of 1 November 1974 and its subsequent resolutions on the question of Cyprus,
Recalling the high-level agreements of 12 February 1977 and 19 May 1979,
Reaffirming the principle of the inadmissibility of occupation and acquisition of territory by force,
Greatly concerned at the prolongation of the Cyprus crisis, which poses a serious threat to international peace and security,
Deeply regretting that the resolutions of the United Nations on Cyprus have not yet been implemented,
Recalling the idea of holding an international conference on Cyprus,
Deploring the fact that part of the territory of the Republic of Cyprus is still occupied by foreign forces,
Deploring the lack of progress in the intercommunal talks,
Deploring all unilateral actions that change the demographic structure of Cyprus or promote faits accomplis,
Reaffirming the need to settle the question of Cyprus without further delay by peaceful means in accordance with the provisions of the Charter of the United Nations and the relevant United Nations resolutions,
1. *Reiterates* its full support for the sovereignty, independence, territorial integrity, unity and non-alignment of the Republic of Cyprus and calls once again for the cessation of all foreign interference in its affairs;
2. *Affirms* the right of the Republic of Cyprus and its people to full and effective sovereignty and control over the entire territory of Cyprus and its natural and other resources and calls upon all States to support and help the Government of the Republic of Cyprus to exercise these rights;
3. *Condemns* any act which tends to undermine the full and effective exercise of the above-mentioned rights, including the unlawful issue of titles of ownership of property;
4. *Welcomes* the proposal for total demilitarization made by the President of the Republic of Cyprus;
5. *Expresses its support* for the high-level agreements of 12 February 1977 and 19 May 1979 and all the provisions thereof;
6. *Demands* the immediate and effective implementation of resolution 3212 (XXIX), unanimously adopted by the General Assembly and endorsed by the Security Council in its resolution 365 (1974) of 13 December 1974, and of the subsequent resolutions of the Assembly and the Council on Cyprus which provide the valid and essential basis for the solution of the problem of Cyprus;

7. *Considers* the withdrawal of all occupation forces from the Republic of Cyprus as an essential basis for a speedy and mutually acceptable solution of the problem of Cyprus;

8. *Demands* the immediate withdrawal of all occupation forces from the Republic of Cyprus;

9. *Commends* the intensification of the efforts made by the Secretary-General, while noting with concern the lack of progress in the intercommunal talks;

10. *Calls* for meaningful, result-oriented, constructive and substantive negotiations between the representatives of the two communities, under the auspices of the Secretary-General, to be conducted freely and on an equal footing, on the basis of relevant United Nations resolutions and the high-level agreements, with a view to reaching as early as possible a mutually acceptable agreement based on the fundamental and legitimate rights of the two communities;

11. *Calls* for respect of the human rights and fundamental freedoms of all Cypriots, including the freedom of movement, the freedom of settlement and the right to property, and the instituting of urgent measures for the voluntary return of the refugees to their homes in safety;

12. *Considers* that the *de facto* situation created by the force of arms should not be allowed to influence or in any way affect the solution of the problem of Cyprus;

13. *Calls upon* the parties concerned to refrain from any unilateral action which might adversely affect the prospects of a just and lasting solution of the problem of Cyprus by peaceful means and to co-operate fully with the Secretary-General in the performance of his task under the relevant resolutions of the General Assembly and the Security Council as well as with the United Nations Peace-keeping Force in Cyprus;

14. *Calls upon* the parties concerned to refrain from any action which violates or is designed to violate the independence, unity, sovereignty and territorial integrity of the Republic of Cyprus;

15. *Reiterates its recommendation* that the Security Council should examine the question of implementation, within a specified time-frame, of its relevant resolutions and consider and adopt thereafter, if necessary, all appropriate and practical measures under the Charter of the United Nations for ensuring the speedy and effective implementation of the resolutions of the United Nations on Cyprus;

16. *Welcomes* the intention of the Secretary-General, as expressed in his report [Doc. A/37/805 of 6/5/1983], to pursue a renewed personal involvement in the quest for a solution of the problem of Cyprus and, in view of this, requests the Secretary-General to undertake such actions or initiatives as he may consider appropriate within the framework of the mission of good offices entrusted to him by the Security Council for promoting a just and lasting solution of the problem and to report to the General Assembly at its thirty-eighth session on the results of his efforts;

17. *Decides* to include the provisional agenda of its thirty-eighth session the item entitled "Question of Cyprus" and requests the Secretary-General to follow up the implementation of the present resolution and to report on all its aspects to the General Assembly at that session.

121st plenary meeting
13 May 1983

[Adopted by 103 votes in favor to 5 against, with 20 abstentions; the votes against were cast by Bangladesh, Malaysia, Pakistan, Somalia, and Turkey.
A separate vote was taken on operative paragraph 8, which was approved by 89 votes in favor to 5 against, with 27 abstentions.
A separate vote was also taken on operative paragraph 15, which was approved by 86 votes in favor to 8 against, with 25 abstentions.]

NOTES

Chapter One

1.   *Cyprus*, Presented to Parliament by the Secretary for the Colonies, the Secretary of State for Foreign Affairs and the Minister of Defence by Command of Her Majesty, July 1960, Cmnd. 1093 (London: Her Majesty's Stationery Office, 1960; reprint, 1964).

2.   Van Coufoudakis, *Cyprus: A Contemporary Problem in Historical Perspective*, Minnesota Mediterranean and East European Monographs, no. 15 (Minneapolis: University of Minnesota, Modern Greek Studies, 2006); and S. A. de Smith, "Cyprus: Sui Generis," in *The New Commonwealth and its Constitutions* (London: Stevens and Sons, 1964), 282-96.

3.   Thomas Ehrlich, "Cyprus: The 'Warlike Isle': Origins and Elements of the Current Crisis," *Stanford Law Review* 18 (May 1966): 1021-98; and Stella Soulioti, *Fettered Independence: Cyprus 1878–1964*, 2 vols. (Minnesota Mediterranean and East European Monographs, no. 16 (Minneapolis: University of Minnesota, Modern Greek Studies, 2006).

4.   UN Security Council resolutions 186 (1964), 187 (1964), 353 (1974), 355 (1974), 541 (1983); and General Assembly resolutions 3212 (XXIX) and 3395 (XXX), among others.

5.   For a detailed discussion of these failed initiatives, see Coufoudakis, *Cyprus: A Contemporary Problem*, 25-42, 82-85.

Chapter Two

1.   David P. Forsythe, *The Internationalization of Human Rights* (Lexington, Mass.: Lexington Books, 1991), 2.

2.   Micheline R. Ishay, *The History of Human Rights* (Berkeley: University of California Press, 2004), 64.

3.   Article 55 is in Chapter IX of the charter which addresses issues of international economic and social cooperation.

4.   For example, the International Covenant on Civil and Political Rights and the International Covenant on Economic, Social and Cultural Rights were adopted in 1966 but did not enter into force until 1976. Similar was the case of the Convention on the Elimination of All Forms of Racial Discrimination. The U.S. opposition to the Genocide Convention is also well documented.

5.   Janne Haaland Matlary, *Intervention for Human Rights in Europe* (New York: Palgrave, 2002), 63.

6.   For example: Greece, 1827, Lebanon, 1860, Crete, 1866, Bulgaria 1873, etc.

7.   Francis G. Jacobs, *The European Convention on Human Rights* (Oxford: Clarendon Press, 1975).

8.   Richard A. Falk, *Human Rights Horizons: The Pursuit of Justice in a Globalizing World* (New York: Routledge, 2000), 2, 7.

9.   The military overthrew the government of Greece in 1967. Democracy was restored in 1974 and Greece resumed its membership in the Council of Europe. A number of interstate applications were filed against Greece by various European countries alleging violations of human rights. On 28 January 1969, the Rapporteur of the Parliamentary Assembly of the Council of Europe determined that Greece violated Article 3 of the convention. Howard D. Coleman, "Greece and the Council of Europe: The International Legal Protection of Human Rights in the Political Process," *Israeli Yearbook of Human Rights* 2 (1972): 121-41.

10.   Jacobs, *The European Convention on Human Rights*, 273-74.

11.   Georghios I. Mintsis, *Οι Διακρατικές Προσφυγές στα Πλίσια της Ευρωπαϊκής Σύμβασης Δικαιωμάτων του Ανθρώπου, Αθήνα-Κομοτηνή* (Interstate applications in the context of the European Convention of Human Rights) (Athens: A. N. Sakkoulas, 2003).

12.   Matlary, *Intervention for Human Rights in Europe*, 123.

13.   J. G. Merrills, *The Development of International Law by the European Court of Human Rights* (Manchester: Manchester University Press, 1993), 2, 12.

14.   Matlary, *Intervention for Human Rights in Europe*, 6-7, 60.

15.   Ibid., 182-84.

16.   An early example of such monitoring and sanction was the "freezing" of the economic association agreement between Greece and the EEC, while Greece was under military rule (1967-74). Van Coufoudakis "The European Economic Community and the 'Freezing' of the Greek Association, 1967–1974," *Journal of Common Market Studies*, 16, no. 2 (December 1977): 114-31.

Chapter Three

1.   Republic of Cyprus, Office of the Law Commissioner, *Index of Treaties of the Republic of Cyprus 1960–2005* (Nicosia: Press and Information Office, 2006).

2.   The former involves day-to-day practical applications of European legal standards in domestic administrative and judicial actions. The latter involves the standards in broad public policy decisions and the adaptation of national legislation to these standards.

3.   Criton G. Tornaritis, "The European Convention of Human Rights in the Legal Order of the Republic of Cyprus," *Cyprus Law Tribune*, 9th year, part 2 (1975).

4.   Applications 176/56 and 299/57.

5.   Council of Europe, European Commission of Human Rights, *Applications 6780/74 and 6950/75, Cyprus against Turkey, Report of the Commission* (Strasbourg, 1976).

6.   The year 1978 had been a period of intense U.S. and UN diplomatic initiatives on Cyprus. It was during 1978 that the Carter administration managed to lift the congressionally imposed arms embargo against Turkey.

7.   Council of Europe, European Commission of Human Rights, *Application No. 25781/94, Cyprus Against Turkey, Report of the Commission, Adopted 4 June 1999* (Strasbourg, 1999).

8.   Recommendation 1576, 23 September 2002; Resolution 1297, 23 September 2002, among others.

9.   Provisions on good neighbor relations, strict observance of the European Convention of Human Rights, implementation of European Court rulings, etc.

10.   A. H. Robertson, *Human Rights in Europe*, 2nd ed. (Manchester: Manchester University Press, 1979), 244-45.

11.   Coufoudakis, *Cyprus: A Contemporary Problem*, 14-21, 25-42, 82-85.

12.   Council of Europe, European Commission of Human Rights, *Decision as to the Admissibility of Application no. 8007/77, Cyprus Against Turkey*, 10 July 1978, paragraph 56.

13.   As amended, both the 1962 Foreign Assistance Act and the 1962 Foreign Military Sales Act call for the reduction and/or suspension of U.S. assistance to countries engaging in a consistent pattern of gross violations of internationally recognized human rights.

14.   For the full text of these resolutions, see Republic of Cyprus, Ministry of Foreign Affairs, *United Nations Security Council and General Assembly Resolutions on Cyprus 1960–2006* (Nicosia: Press and Information Office, 2006); and Republic of Cyprus, Press and Information Office, *European Stand on the Cyprus Problem* (Nicosia: Press and Information Office, 2003).

Chapter Four

1.   President Makarios of Cyprus escaped assassination during the 15 July 1974 coup. He managed to reach the British bases in Cyprus where he was given refuge and assisted in leaving Cyprus for his safety. Soon after the Turkish invasion of Cyprus began, the junta ruling Greece collapsed and so did the puppet regime it had installed in Nicosia. Glafkos Clerides, speaker of the House of Representatives, assumed the position of acting president under the 1960 Constitution until the return of President Makarios to Cyprus in November 1974.

2.   On 13 February 1975, Turkey created the so-called "Turkish Federated State of Cyprus" in the occupied areas. On 15 November 1983, the so-called "Assembly" of the "Turkish Federated State of Cyprus" unilaterally declared its independence from the Republic of Cyprus and proclaimed itself as the "Turkish Republic of Northern Cyprus." Turkey is the only country to recognize this secessionist entity. All of the international community recognizes only the 1960-established Republic of Cyprus.

3.   On this, see Ian Brownlie, "The Prohibition of the Use of Armed Force for the Solution of International Differences with Particular Reference to the Affairs of the Republic of Cyprus," *International Law Conference on Cyprus 1979*, ed. Cyprus Bar Council (Nicosia: Cyprus Bar Council, 1981), 198-226; Belma Bayar, *British, Greek and Turkish Views on the Interpretation of the Treaty of Guarantee of 1960* (Washington, D.C.: Library of Congress, 1990); and Kypros Chrysostomides, *The Republic of Cyprus: A Study in International Law* (The Hague: Martin Nijhoff Publishers, 1990), 117-58.

4.   Article II of the 1960 Treaty of Guarantee and Article 185 of the constitution.

5.   Including Cypriots of Armenian, Maronite, and Latin heritage, since under the 1960 Constitution, all three communities are considered to be part of the Greek Cypriot community.

6.   For example, paragraph 503 in the decision on the interstate application 6780/74 and 6950/75; paragraphs 161 and 162 in 8007/77, and paragraphs 173, 174, 309, and 310 in 25781/94.

7.   Council of Europe, European Court of Human Rights, Decision by the Fourth Section of the European Court of Human Rights on the Admissibility of Application 28940/95 by Eleni Foka against Turkey, 9 November 2006. For the judgment of the Fourth Section, see European Court of Human Rights, Fourth Section, Case of Foka v. Turkey, Application No. 28940/95, Judgment, 24 Juna 2008.

8.   *Cyprus v. Turkey*, 25781/1994, paragraphs 75-81.

9.   Referred to as the 4th Geneva Convention in this text.

10.   United Nations, Economic and Social Council, Commission on Human Rights, 11 August 2005, E/CN.4/Sub.2/2005/L11/Add.2, pp. 1-2.

11.   The negative vote was that of the Turkish member of the commission.

12.   Council of Europe, European Commission of Human Rights, Application No. 25781/94, *Cyprus Against Turkey, Report of the Commission*, Strasbourg, 4 June 1999. The case was referred to the European Court of Human Rights. European Court of Human Rights, Case of Cyprus v. Turkey, application 25781/94, Judgment, 10 May 2001.

13.   See paragraphs 172, 174, 188, 193, and 194.

14.   For example, 361(1974), paragraphs 4 and 5 in particular; 774 (1992) preamble.

15.   For example, 3212(XXIX), 1 November 1974, operative paragraph 5; 3395 (XXX), 20 November 1975, operative paragraph 4; 34/30, 20 November 1979, operative paragraph 7; 37/253, 13 May 1983, operative paragraph 11, among others.

16.   Recommendations 737(1974); 756 (1975); and 1056(1987), among others.

17.   Resolution, 12 September 1991, paragraph C, among others.

18.   For example, resolution 4(XXXII), 27 February 1976, paragraph 1; resolution 17 (XXXIV), 7 March 1978, paragraph 1; resolution 1987/50, 11 March 1987, paragraphs 1 and 4, among others.

19.   Judgment, application 25781/94, 10 May 2001, paragraph 5, section III, p. 95; paragraph 19, section IV, p. 98.

20.   6780/74 and 6950/75, pp. 120-24 in particular.

21.   Report of Asme-Humanitas Delegation Concerning Cyprus v. Turkey, Asme-Humanitas, e.v, Iphofen/Ufr, Federal Republic of Germany, p. 35.

22.   During the course of 2007, undocumented rumors surfaced once more about the use of Greek Cypriot POWs in Turkish chemical and bacteriological weapons tests. These POWs had been in Turkish custody but were never released after the cessation of hostilities and the prisoner exchange.

23.   The text of these resolutions is included in Republic of Cyprus, Press and Information Office, *European Stand on the Cyprus Problem* (Nicosia: PIO, 2003), 92-95.

Chapter Five

1.   The number of Greek Cypriot missing is .26 percent of the total population in 1974. In contrast, the number of U.S. servicemen listed missing in Vietnam in 1975 was .004 percent of the U.S. population.

2.   Paul Saint Cassia, "Missing Persons in Cyprus as *Ethnomartyres*," *Modern Greek Studies Yearbook* 14/15 (1998/1999): 261-84.

3.   Pan-Cyprian Committee of Parents and Relatives of Undeclared Prisoners of War and Missing Persons, *Disappearances: The Case of the Missing Cypriots* (Nicosia: Pan-Cyprian Committee . . .), 1990.

4.   This was the case of Andrew Kasapis, a sixteen-year-old American of Cypriot origin. He was apprehended and killed during the invasion. The missing Americans became the object of a resolution adopted by the U.S. Senate on 5 October 1994. President Clinton appointed Ambassador Dillon to investigate the Kasapis case. His grave was located in the occupied areas in January 1998 and his remains were returned to the United States on 22 June 1998. A legitimate question can be raised as to why Turkey cooperated in this one case only and not in the other cases of missing Greek Cypriots.

5.   United Nations Press Release, Office of Public Information, Press Section, CYP/1061, 22 April 1981.

6.   Some witnesses were afraid of self-incrimination while others were afraid of reprisals. A report in Turkish Cypriot daily *Afrika*, 9 December 2006, indicated that a "Turkish Revenge Brigade" threatened not only CMP members and members of the CMP team, but also the villagers of the Chatez village in the occupied areas where exhumations were to take place. The villagers were threatened with death notices placed under the doors of their homes.

7.   Cyprus News Agency, 8 August 2007.

8.   Applications 16064/90, 16065/90, 16066/90, 16068/90, 16069/90, 16070/90, 16071/90, 16072/90, and 16073/90. Under the new court format, the court breaks up in sections. Not all cases are in plenary session; this is why these cases were 6-1 votes.

9.   Typical are resolutions 1146(1997); 1283(1999); 1569(2004); and 1687(2006), among others.

10.   Such as: 3450(xxx) of 9 December 1975; 32/128 of 16 December 1977; and 33/181 of 17 December 1982, among others.

11.   Such as: 4(xxxi), 4(xxxii), 17(xxxiv), 1987/50

12.   The largest number of the enclaved live in the village of Rizokarpasso (some 261 persons) and Ayia Triada (approximately 102 persons), both in the Karpass Peninsula. The village of Kormakitis located west of Kyrenia was the largest of the Maronite villages, with some 108 persons living there. The rest are spread among other small hamlets and villages.

13.   For the text of the communiqué, see: Republic of Cyprus, Press and Information Office, Documents, "The Third Vienna Agreement," 2 August 1975.

14.   Yannakis M. Moussas, *Εγκλωβισμένοι: Μια Θλιβερή Πραγματικότητα* (Enclaved: A sad reality) (Nicosia: PIO, 1993), 27-29.

15.   No. 28940/95, Eleni Foka against Turkey.

16.   Ibid., p. 36.

17.   CommDH(2004) 2.

18.   Document no. 9714.

19.   For example: 1682 (2002); 1297(2002); and 1576(2002).

20.   Interim Resolution DH(2005)44.

21.   The text of the recommendations has also been reprinted in: Republic of Cyprus, Press and Information Office, *The Cyprus Question* (Nicosia: PIO, 2003), 80-82.

22.   European Court of Human Rights, *Cyprus v. Turkey*, Application No. 25781/94, Judgment, 10 May 2001, par. 304.

Chapter Six

1.   As in the case of Loizidou against Turkey.

2.   "Law" 67/2005 for the Compensation, Exchange and Restitution of Immovable Property.

3.   This law attempted to provide effective domestic remedies for indemnifying Kurdish victims of the armed conflict between Turkish security forces and the Kurdish PKK rebels. See the report by Human Rights Watch, No. 1, December 2006, "Unjust, Restrictive and Inconsistent: The Impact of Turkey's Compensation Law With Respect to Internally Displaced People."

4.   Note that iron, cement, and bricks are primary building materials in Cyprus. These figures must be seen in relation to the population of the occupied areas which, by 2005, had reached approximately 240,000, of whom only about 82,000 were Turkish Cypriots. In addition, there were approximately 40,000 Turkish troops stationed in occupied Cyprus.

5.   Characteristic is the letter by Ambassador George Zotiades to the Israeli paper *Ha'aretz*, 19 September 2006.

6.   Applications 6780/74 and 6950/75.

7.   Application 8007/77.

8.   Application 25781/94.

9.   Comm DH(2004)2, Strasbourg, 12 February 2004.

10.   E/CN.4/Sub.2/2005/L.11/Add.2.

11.   Report on the Demographic Structure of the Cypriot Communities, 27 April 1992, Parliamentary Assembly, Doc. 6589, paragraph 106.

12.   Claire Palley, *An International Relations Debacle* (Oxford and Portland, Ore.: Hart Publishing, 2005), 67-79.

13.   Such as: 33/15(1978); 24/30(1979); and 37/253(1983).

14.   Such as: 4(xxxii) 1976; 1987/50.

15.   "Cultural Heritage of Cyprus," Strasbourg, 2 July 1989, AS/Cult/AA(41), 1.

16.   Ibid., 3.

17.   "The Rape of Northern Cyprus," *The Guardian* (London), 6 May 1976.

18.   Michael Jansen, "Cyprus: The Loss of a Cultural Heritage," *Modern Greek Studies Yearbook* 2 (1986): 323.

19.   In a series of articles in the Turkish Cypriot weekly magazine *Olay*, 26 April–17 May 1982. See also Jansen, "Cyprus,' 318-19; and Michael Jansen, *War and Cultural Heritage: Cyprus after the 1974 Turkish Invasion*, Minnesota Mediterranean and East European Monographs, no. 14 (Minneapolis: University of Minnesota, Modern Greek Studies, 2005), 27-28.

20.   "Cultural Heritage of Cyprus," 21.

21.   For example, the Monastery of St. Barnabas, the founder of the Church of Cyprus, the Monastery of St. Andrew in the Karpass Peninsula, the church in the Bellapais Abbey, and the Church of St. Anastasia in Lapithos. The author has visited all these sites.

22.   An excellent recent source is a book by the Rev. D. Demosthenous, *Churches of Occupied Cyprus* (Nicosia: Monastery of Kykkos Research Centre, 2006). The book contains a good pictorial record and commentary on the significance of these religious sites.

23.   In her book *War and Cultural Heritage*, Michael Jansen minutely documents the ties of Turkish Cypriot, Turkish, and other black marketeers in the case of these mosaics (29-70). The decision of the U.S. Court of Appeals for the 7th Circuit, 917 F. 2d278, Autocephalous Greek Orthodox Church of Cyprus v. Goldberg and Feldman Fine Arts Inc., is dated 24 October 1990.

24.   For example, the twenty-year agreement with the Menil Foundation of Houston, Texas, in the United States (see Jansen, *War and Cultural Heritage*, 37-39).

25.   Resolution, 10 March 1988, paragraphs 9a,b 10, 11, 12; Resolution, 15 December 1988, specifically condemning the destruction of Cypriot cultural heritage in the territory occupied by Turkey; Resolution, 27 March 1996, paragraph G; and Resolution, 5 September 2001, paragraph K, among others.

GLOSSARY

Agnooumenoi	Greek Cypriot missing persons, both civilian and military, following the 1974 Turkish invasion of Cyprus
Annan V	fifth version of the arbitration plan for the resolution of the Cyprus problem proposed by former UN secretary-general Kofi Annan in March 2004; Greek Cypriots rejected this plan by a vote of 76 percent in the referendum of 24 April 2004
CMP	Committee on Missing Persons
COE	Council of Europe
EAAF	Argentine Forensic Anthropology Team involved in the identification of the remains of Cypriot missing persons
ECHR	European Convention of Human Rights
EComHR	European Commission of Human Rights
ECtHR	European Court of Human Rights
EU	European Union; earlier, the EEC (European Economic Community)
ICRC	International Committee of the Red Cross
MIA	missing in action
NGO	nongovernmental organization
OSCE	Organization for Security and Cooperation in Europe; formerly known as the Conference on Security and Cooperation in Europe (CSCE; 1975)
POW	prisoner of war

"TFSC"   so-called "Turkish Federated State of Cyprus," an illegal entity created in occupied Cyprus by the Turkish army in 1975

"TRNC"   so-called "Turkish Republic of Northern Cyprus," the illegal entity that succeeded the "TFSC" on 15 November 1983; created by the Turkish army, this illegal entity has been in violation of resolutions by the UN Security Council

UDHR   the 1948 United Nations "Universal Declaration of Human Rights"

UN   the United Nations (1945)

UNFICYP   the United Nations Peacekeeping Force in Cyprus (1964)

BIBLIOGRAPHY

In the interest of space, the note references are not included in this selective bibliography.

Amnesty International. *Cyprus-Missing Persons in Cyprus-Amnesty International's Actions 1974–1989*. London: International Secretariat, August 1989.

Andrews, J. A., and W. D. Hines. *Key Guide to Information Sources on the International Protection of Human Rights*. New York: Facts on File, 1987.

Athanassiades, Spyros, "Turkish Settlers in Occupied North" In *Cyprus Yearbook 1994*, 79-84. Nicosia: KYKEM, 1995.

Blackburn, Robert, ed. *The ECHR: The Impact of the ECHR in the Legal and Political System of Member States*. New York: Cassell, 1996.

Castberg, Fred. *The European Convention of Human Rights*. Leiden: A. W. Sijtoft, 1974.

Centre on Housing Rights and Evictions. *The Pinheiro Principles: UN Principles on Housing and Property Restitution for Refugees and Displaced Persons*. Geneva: COHRE, 2006.

Chotzakoglou, Charalampos G. *Religious Monuments in Turkish-Occupied Cyprus: Evidence and Acts of Continuous Destruction*. Studies in Byzantine and Ost-Byzantine Archaeology and History of Art, no. 3. Nicosia: Museum of the Holy Monastery of Kykkos, 2008.

Chrysostomides, Daphne. *Les Requêtes Cypriotes Contre la Turquie Devant la Commission et la Cour Européenne des Droits de l'Homme et leur Importance*. Nicosia, 1998.

Committee for the Protection of the Cultural Heritage of Cyprus. *Cyprus: A Civilization Plundered*. Athens: The Hellenic Parliament, 2002.

Conference on Security and Cooperation in Europe. *Report of the CSCE Meeting of Experts on National Minorities, July 1–19, 1992*. International Legal Materials, 30 November 1992, 1692-1702.

Coufoudakis, Van. "Cyprus and the European Convention on Human Rights: The Law and Politics of Cyprus v. Turkey, Applications 6780/74 and 6950/75." *Human Rights Quarterly* 4, no. 4 (1982): 450-73, 497-507.

Council of Europe, Office of the Commissioner of Human Rights, The Commissioner of Human Rights. *Report by Mr. Alvaro Gil-Robles on his Visit to Cyprus 25–29 June 2003, to the Attention of the Committee of Ministers and of the Parliamentary Assembly, Strasbourg, 12 February*

2004, Comm DH (2004) 2 and *Follow-up Report on Cyprus (2003–2005) for the Attention of the Committee of Ministers and the Parliamentary Assembly.* Strasbourg, 29 March 2006, Comm DH (2006) 12.

Court of Justice of the European Communities. *Judgment of the Court, 5 July 1994: EEC-Cyprus Association Agreement.* Case C-432192.

Cyprus Bar Association. *Human Rights: Turkey's Violations of Human Rights in Cyprus: Findings of the European Court of Human Rights and Continuing Violations by Turkey.* Nicosia: Cyprus Bar Association, 1995.

Delperee, Francis. "Principles of Federation and the Protection of Human Rights in Relation to Proposals for the Constitutional Structure of Cyprus." In *International Law Conference on Cyprus-1979,* ed. Cyprus Bar Council, 157-97. Nicosia: Cyprus Bar Council, 1981.

Evdokas, Takis. *Refugees of Cyprus: A Representative Socio-Psychological Study.* Nicosia: Socio-Psychological Group, 1976.

———. *Πρόσφυγες της Κύπρου: Αντιπροσωπευτική έρευνα αναμεσα στις 200,000* (Refugees of Cyprus: Representative investigation among 200,000). Nicosia: Theopress, 1976.

Fawcett, J. E. S. *The Application of the European Convention of Human Rights.* Oxford: Oxford University Press, 1987.

Fisher, Jo-Ann. *Mothers of the Disappeared.* London: Zed Books, 1989.

Forsythe, David P. *The International Protection of Human Rights.* New York: Lexington Books, 1991.

———. *Human Rights in the New Europe.* University of Nebraska Press, 1994.

Free United Karpas Association. *The Enclaved in the Occupied Area of Cyprus.* Nicosia: Free United Karpas Association, 1993.

Glendon, M. A. *Rights Talk: The Impoverishment of Political Discourse.* New York: Free Press, 1991.

Hannum, Hurst. *Autonomy, Sovereignty and Self Determination: The Accommodation of Conflicting Rights.* Philadelphia: University of Pennsylvania Press, 1990.

Hannum, Hurst, ed. *Guide to International Human Rights Practice.* Ardsley, N.Y.: Transnational Publications, 1999.

Hellenic Information Committee. *The European Human Rights Commission Condemns the Turkish Atrocities in Cyprus.* Athens: n.p., 1977

Henkin, Louis, ed. *International Bill of Rights: Covenant on Civil and Political Rights.* New York: Columbia University Press, 1981.

Hoving, Thomas. "How to Acquire a Stolen Masterpiece." *Connoisseur* (November 1998): 218-20.

Human Rights Watch. "Unjust, Restrictive and Inconsistent: The Impact of Turkey's Compensation Law With Respect to Internally Displaced People." No.1 (December 2006).

Ioannides, Christos. *In Turkey's Image: The Transformation of Occupied Cyprus into a Turkish Province.* New Rochelle, N.Y.: A. D. Caratzas Publishers, 1991.

———. "Changing the Demography of Cyprus: Anatolian Settlers in the Turkish Occupied North." In *Cyprus: Domestic Dynamics—External*

Constraints, 19-44. New Rochelle, N.Y.: A. D. Caratzas Publishers, 1992.

Jansen, Michael. *War and Cultural Heritage: Cyprus after the 1974 Turkish Invasion*. Minnesota Mediterranean and East European Monographs, no. 14. Minneapolis: University of Minnesota, Modern Greek Studies, 2005.

King, Russel. "Cypriot Refugees in Cyprus South of the Attila Line." *Geographical Magazine*, no. 52 (1980): 226-73.

Kline, Thomas. "Beyond Diplomacy: Protecting the Cultural Heritage of Cyprus." In *The United States and Cyprus: Double Standards and the Rule of Law*, ed. Eugene Rossides and Van Coufoudakis, 343-45. Washington, D.C.: AHIF, 2002.

Loizos, Peter. *The Heart Grown Bitter: A Chronicle of Cypriot War Refugees*. New York: Cambridge University Press, 1982.

Loukaides, Loukis G. "Colloquy-Democracy and Human Rights." Paper presented at the Conference on Written Communication on Human Rights and Foreign Policy, Council of Europe, H/Coll (87) 11. Strasbourg, 1987.

————. "The Protection of Human Rights Pending the Settlement of Related Political Issues." *The British Yearbook of International Law* 58 (1987): 349-59.

————. "The Judgment of the European Court of Human Rights in the Case of Cyprus v. Turkey." *Leiden Journal of International Law* 15 (2002): 225-36.

Macris, Nicolas D., ed. *The 1960 Treaties on Cyprus and Selected Subsequent Acts*. Manheim: Bibliopolis, 2003.

Mastny, Votech. *Helsinki, Human Rights and European Security*. Durham, N.C.: Duke University Press, 1986.

Mavromatis, Andreas. "Peaceful Settlement of Disputes, Human Rights and the Question of Cyprus." In *Cyprus-Yearbook 1994*, 79-84. Nicosia: KYKEM, 1995.

Meyer, William H. "American Interests and the Crisis in Cyprus: A Human Rights Perspective." *The Cyprus Review* 5, no. 1 (1993): 2-27.

Mintsis, Georgios. "The Human Rights Protection in the Framework of the Organization on Security and Cooperation in Europe." *Balkan Studies* 32 (1997): 325-53.

Nickel, J. W. *Making Sense of Human Rights: Philosophical Reflections on the Universal Declaration of Human Rights*. Berkeley: University of California Press, 1987.

Pan Cyprian Association for the Protection of Human Rights. *The Continuing Violations of Human Rights by Turkey in Cyprus*. Nicosia: Theo Press, 2003.

Peterson, John, and Michael Shackleton. *The Institutions of the European Union*. 2nd ed. Oxford: Oxford University Press, 2006.

Pollis, Adamantia. "The Missing of Cyprus: A Distinctive Case." *Journal of Modern Greek Studies* 9 (1991): 44-62.

Robinson, Mary. *Human Rights and Ethical Globalization.* San Diego, Calif.: University of San Diego, Joan B. Kroc Institute for Peace and Justice, 2005.

Rossides, Eugene T. "Cyprus and the Rule of Law." *Syracuse Journal of International Law and Commerce* 17, no. 1 (spring 1991): 21-90.

Rossides, Eugene T. "The Rule of Law and Human Rights in International Affairs." In *Cyprus Yearbook 1994*, 11-36. Nicosia: KYKEM, 1995.

Republic of Cyprus, Press and Information Office. *Report of the United Nations Mediator on Cyprus Mr. Galo Plaza to the Secretary-General, 26 March 1965.* Nicosia: PIO, 1965.

———. *An Authentic Study and Documentation of the Violations of Human Rights in Cyprus by Turkey: The Truth and the Facts.* Nicosia: PIO, 1975.

———. "Plundering of the Cypriot Cultural Heritage in Occupied Cyprus." Nicosia: PIO, 1988.

———. *International Condemnation of the Turkish Cypriot Pseudostate.* Nicosia: PIO, 1989.

———. *The Cyprus Refugee Problem: Humanitarian Aspects.* Nicosia: PIO, 1989.

———. *Turkish Demographic Manipulation in Cyprus.* Nicosia: PIO, 1989.

———. *Κύπρος και το Συμβούλιο της Ευρώπης 1949–1999* (Cyprus and the Council of Europe 1949–1999). Nicosia: PIO, 1999.

———. *The Cyprus Question.* Nicosia: PIO, 2003.

Sant Cassia, Paul. *Bodies of Evidence: Burial, Memory and the Recovery of Missing Persons in Cyprus.* Oxford; Berghahn Books, 2005.

Scheffer, David J. "Cyprus: International Law and the Role of the United Nations." Testimony before the Subcommittee on European Affairs, Committee on Foreign Relations, U.S. Senate, April 17, 1991.

———. "Human Rights and the New World Order: The Relevance of Cyprus." *Modern Greek Studies Yearbook* 8 (1992): 207-19.

Shapiro, I., and W. Kymlicka, eds. *Ethnicity and Group Rights.* New York: New York University Press, 1997.

Sohn, Louis B., and Thomas Buergenthal, eds. *International Protection of Human Rights.* Indianapolis, Ind.: Bobbs Merrill, 1973.

Tarr, Alan G. "Cyprus and the Clash of Rights." *Indian Journal of Federal Studies*, no. 1 (2003): 16-27.

Tirman, John. "Human Rights in Cyprus." In *The United States and Cyprus-Double Standards and the Rule of Law*, ed. Eugene T. Rossides and Van Coufoudakis, 343-45. Washington, D.C.: AHIF, 2002.

Tornaritis, Criton G. "Legal Aspects of Refugees in Cyprus." *Cyprus Law Tribune*, 9th year, pt. 2 (1975): 21-38.

———. "Violations of Human Rights During Military Action." *Cyprus Law Tribune*, 9th year, pt. 2 (1975): 39-62.

———. *The Turkish Invasion of Cyprus and Legal Problems Arising Therefrom.* Nicosia: Printing Office of the Republic of Cyprus, 1975.

United Kingdom. In the High Court of Justice, Queens Bench Division, Case No. QB/2005/PTA/0897, 9/6/2006 Before Mr. Justice Black, Between

David Charles Orams and Linda Elizabeth Orams, appellants, and Meletios Apostolides, respondent, approved judgment.

United Nations. *Bulletin of Human Rights. Special Issue: Fortieth Anniversary of the Universal Declaration of Human Rights*. Geneva: United Nations, 1988.

United Nations, Department of Public Information. *The United Nations and Human Rights, 1945–1995*. New York: United Nations, 1995.

United Nations, Economic and Social Council, Commission on Human Rights, Sub-Commission on Protection and Promotion of Human Rights, 57th session, E/CN.4/Sub.2/2005/L.11/Add.2, 11 August 2005. *Draft Report of the Sub-Commission on the Promotion and Protection of Human Rights*. Rapporteur Yozo Yokota.

United States, Department of State. *Country Reports on Human Rights Practices*. Report Submitted to the Committee on Foreign Affairs, U.S. House of Representatives and to the Committee on Foreign Affairs, U.S. Senate by the Department of State. Annual Edition.

Van Rijn, Michel. *Hot Art, Cold Cash*. London: Little Brown, 1993.

Zetter, Robert. "Refugees and Forced Migrants as Development Resources: The Greek Cypriot Refugees from 1974." *The Cyprus Review* 3, no. 2, 7-39.

INDEX

Page locators for notes (n.) include page number followed by chapter: note (i.e., 119 n. 5:4).

Acar, Ozgen, 85
Accession to the European Union, Treaty of (2003), 2
Achaean Greeks, 5
Achna (village), 45
acquis communautaire, 2, 28
"agnooumenoi", 49
agricultural production, 4, 42
Akinci, Mustafa, 83
Amnesty International, 49–50
Amsterdam Treaty, 12–13
Annan, Kofi, 17, 37, 91, 93
Annan V Plan (2004), 17–18, 22–23, 69–71, 74, 82–83, 91–93
Apostolides, Meletios, 78–79
Apostolos Andreas (monastery), 60, 65
archaeological sites, 4, 42, 74, 84–90
Archbishop Makarios III, 117 n. 4:1
Argentine Forensic Anthropology Team (EAAF), 53
Armenian minorities, 35, 61, 86–87, 118 n. 4:5
Asme-Humanitas report, 44, 46, 66–67
Asomatos (village), 61
Australia, Greek Cypriot migration to, 4, 37
Ayia Marina (village), 61
Ayia Triada (village), 120 n. 5:12

Balkans, 14, 22
Bellapais Abbey, 86, 121 n. 6:21
Berlin Declaration (1957), 12

biological weapons testing, 119 n. 4:22
"bi-zonal bicommunal federation", 37
black-market sales of antiquities, 4, 86–90, 121 n. 6:23
Blair, Tony, 70
Booth, Cherie, 70
Bosnia, 39
Burns, Nicholas, 89–90
Byzantine Empire (330–1191 A.D.), 5, 86, 90
Byzantine Icons Museum, 88

Carter, Jimmy, 117 n. 3:6
Cassin, Rene, 8
Charalambous, Demetris Koutras, 53
Charter of Fundamental Freedoms (EU), 2, 15
Charter of Fundamental Rights (EU, 2000), 13, 37, 69–70
Chatez (village), 119 n. 5:6
Chatzakoglou (Dr.), 89
Chechnya, 14
chemical weapons testing, 119 n. 4:22
children, 43–46, 62–66. *See also* families and society
Church of Antiphonitis, 88
Church of Cyprus, 88–89, 121 n. 6:21
Church of Kanakaria, 88
Church of St. Anastasia, 86–87, 121 n. 6:21

churches and cultural heritage. *See* religion/religious minorities

Clerides, Glafkos, 117 n. 4:1

Clinton, William J., 119 n. 5:4

Cold War: emergence of human rights regimes, 12–14; ethnic cleansing, 35; post-WWII human rights and, 7–9

colonialism: Cyprus as British territory, 5, 16–17; post-WWII human rights and, 7

colonization, Turkish policy of, 4, 81–84

Committee of Ministers, Council of Europe, 10–12, 58–59, 67–68

Committee on Missing Persons, 51–53, 119 n. 5:6. *See also* missing persons

community and society: Cypriot customs and tradition, 50; of "enclaved" Cypriots, 60–68; impact of invasion on, 4; invasion damage to, 36–37. *See also* ethnic cleansing

concentration camps, 46

Conference on Security and Cooperation in Europe (CSCE), 14–15

confiscation of property: addressing the issue of, 69–71; addressing Turkish violations, 20; documented evidence of, 73–74; "domestic remedies law", 71–73, 120 n. 6:2; of "enclaved" Cypriots, 62–64; following invasion, 4; international response to, 79–81; pending court cases, 17–18; seizure and destruction, 41–42. *See also* ethnic cleansing; property rights/law

Constitution of Cyprus (1960), 1, 31–32, 61, 75, 117 n. 4:1, 118 n. 4:5

Cormack, Robin, 85

Council of Europe: creation of, 9–14; Cyprus resolutions, 26–29, 37–39, 92; human rights, 6–7

Crusades, 5

Cuco, Alfons, 81, 84

cultural heritage: destruction following invasion, 4; ethnic cleansing by destruction of, 69, 84–86; Hellenic history and, 5, 86–87; official complicity in destruction of, 87–88; protection and recovery of artifacts, 88–90; Turkish colonization policy, 81–83

cultural imperialism, 7

Cyprus: dealing with human rights in, 5–6; ethnic minorities, 35, 61; history and culture to 1878, 5; impact of invasion, 2–5; independence from Britain, 1, 91; status quo ante, 2, 31–33

Cyprus, Republic of: as "bi-zonal bicommunal federation", 37; Constitution of 1960, 31–32, 75, 117 n. 4:1, 118 n. 4:5; coup by Greek junta, 2, 31–32, 51–52, 117 n. 4:1; EU membership, 2, 5, 15–16, 21–22, 93; human rights violations in, 11–12, 18–21; international support of, 26–29; protection of property rights, 74–75; Treaty of Establishment (1960), 84; tri-partite independence agreement, 1, 17; UN membership, 15–16. *See also* Greek Cypriots; intercommunal relations; Turkish Cypriots

Cyprus: A Contemporary Problem in Historical Perspective (Coufoudakis), 91

Cyprus Constitution of 1960, 2

Cyprus Problem/Question: background for understanding the, 5–6; current status of, 91–93; foundation for settling, 31; human rights and, 21–24; internationalization of, 25–29;

redefining the, 51; Turkish colonization policy, 82–84

Dalibard, Jacques, 88
de Zayas, Alfred, 80
Declaration of Independence (America, 1776), 7
Declaration of the Rights of Man and the Citizen (France, 1878), 7
Demades v. Turkey, 78
Denktash, Rauf, 50, 58
deportation of civilians, 4, 35–36, 38–40
detainees/detention, 4, 36, 40, 44–47
Dillon, Robert, 119 n. 5:4
discrimination: EU protections from, 13–14; Turkish violations in Cyprus, 33–35. *See also* ethnic cleansing
displaced persons/refugees: addressing Turkish violations, 20; dealing with the problems of, 36–39; following invasion, 4; property rights of, 69–71; Turkish colonization policy, 84. *See also* "enclaved" Cypriots; forced evacuation/migration; missing persons
"domestic remedies law", 71–73, 120 n. 6:2

economic development/reconstruction: destruction of historic sites, 87; following invasion, 4, 36–37; property confiscation/usurpation, 73–81
Eleni Foka v. Turkey, 34, 66
employment rights, 13
"enclaved" Cypriots: addressing the issue of, 60, 68; choosing safety vs. home, 62; court decisions on fate of, 65–66; international response to, 66–68; living conditions of, 63–65; Maronite Cypriots, 61; property rights, 70–71; Third Vienna Agree-

ment, 61; Turkish colonization policy, 83
English Bill of Rights (1689), 7
Eptakomi (village), 53
ethnic cleansing: addressing evidence of, 35–36, 39–40, 47; destruction of cultural heritage, 69, 84–86; Maronite Cypriots, 61; politics and legitimization of, 22, 26, 34–35; resulting from invasion, 3, 31–32. *See also* community and society; families and society
ethnic cleansing techniques: confiscation of property, 17–18; deprivation of home and possessions, 41–42; destruction, robbery, looting, 42; displacement and partitioning, 36–39; false detention, deprivation of liberty, 46; rape and forced prostitution, 43; separation of families, 40–41; torture, inhuman treatment, murder, 43–46
ethnic minorities, 8–9. *See also* Armenian minorities; Maronite Cypriots
"Europa Nostra", 85
European Commission on Human Rights: British violations in Cyprus, 16–17; Cyprus resolutions, 26–29; determinations regarding Turkey, 4; evidence of ethnic cleansing, 35–47; human rights mandate, 9–14; on missing persons issue, 53–59; Turkish violations in Cyprus, 33–34
European Convention: Cyprus membership, 15–16; Cyprus resolutions, 26–29; establishment of Protocols, 9–10; on missing persons issue, 53–59; on right to property, 69–70; Turkish violations of, 2, 4, 18–21, 33–35; violation and appeal procedure, 10–11;

violations and non-compliance decisions, 11–12
European Court of Human Rights (1959): creation of, 9–14; Cyprus resolutions, 26–29, 92; "domestic remedies law", 71–73, 120 n. 6:2; "enclaved" Cypriot cases, 65–68; evidence of ethnic cleansing, 35–39; *Loizidou v. Turkey*, 20–21; missing persons issue, 50; Turkey defiance of, 21–22
European Court of Justice, 13
European Economic Community (EEC), 11, 13–16, 116 n. 2:16
European Ministers of Foreign Affairs, 11
European Parliament: Cyprus resolutions, 28, 37–39, 67–68, 92; human rights role, 13; missing persons issue, 57–58
European Social Charter (1965), 10, 13
European Union: creation of, 12–14; Cyprus accession to membership, 2, 5, 15–16, 21; Cyprus as second-class member, 91–92; Cyprus resolutions, 26–29; dealing with the Cyprus Question, 5–6; Turkey accession negotiations, 2, 5, 12–13, 21
European Union Defense network, 1

false detention. *See* detainees/ detention
Famagusta (city), 4, 78
families and society: displacement of, 38–39; of "enclaved" Cypriots, 62–64; impact of invasion on, 4; missing persons as issue for, 49–51, 57; reunification plans, 61; separation of, 40–41. *See also* ethnic cleansing
Fielding, J., 85
Foka, Eleni, 34, 66

forced evacuation/migration: ethnic cleansing by, 35–40; following invasion, 4. *See also* displaced persons/refugees
foreign military bases, 1, 4, 45, 117 n. 4:1. *See also* Turkish Army
Founding Treaty (EEC), 13
France, 7, 89
Fundamental Rights Agency (EU, 2007), 13–14

Geneva Conventions (1949): killing of civilians and captives, 51; missing persons, 54, 58; protection of civilians, 31–32, 35–36; protection of property, 80, 83; on resettlement, 4; torture and protection of women, 43–44
genocide, 8–9, 39
Genocide Convention, 115 n. 2:4
Georgiou, Christakis, 53
Germany: Asme-Humanitas report, 44, 46, 66–67; investment/ development in Cyprus, 73–74; Nuremberg War Crimes Trial (1945), 8; Turkish Cypriot migration to, 4
Gil-Robles, Alvaro, 67, 80
Girod, Christophe, 53
Gobbi, Hugo J., 51
Great Britain: Cyprus as colony, 5; Cyprus independence agreement, 1, 17; deportation of refugees, 39; English Bill of Rights (1689), 7; failure to act in Cyprus, 37, 45; human rights violations, 34–35; Inforce Foundation, 53; investment/development in Cyprus, 73–74, 79; involvement in Cyprus Problem, 18–19, 22, 91; migration by Greek Cypriots, 37; migration by Turkish Cypriots, 4; military bases in Cyprus, 1, 4, 45, 117 n. 4:1; recovery of antiquities, 89
Greece: Cypriot independence agreement, 1, 17; Cyprus coup

by ruling junta, 2, 31–32, 51–52, 117 n. 4:1; foreign policy and security issues, 115 n. 2:4; history and culture in Cyprus, 5; membership in Council of Europe, 10, 116 n. 2:9; under military rule, 116 n. 2:9, 117 n. 4:1

Greek Cypriots: accounting for missing persons, 50–53; Annan V Plan, 23; anti-colonial rebellion, 16–17; ethnic cleansing of, 35–39; forced expulsion, 3; property rights, 69–71; as target for Turkish actions, 31–33; Third Vienna Agreement (1975), 61; tri-partite independence agreement, 1, 17; Turkish actions toward, 33–34

Greek Orthodox Church. *See* religion/religious minorities

"Grey Wolves", 45

Guberan, Pierre, 53

Gypsou (detention camp), 46

Hague Convention (1907), 80

Hellenic history. *See* cultural heritage

Helsinki Final Act (1975), 14–15, 57–58

High Commissioner of Human Rights, 10

history to 1878. *See* cultural heritage

human rights: background for understanding the, 5–6; evidence of violations, 31–33; foundation and history of, 7–9; politics as determinant in, 18–26; sanctions and results, 47; Turkish invasion of Cyprus and, 2–6; violation and appeal procedure, 10–12

Human Rights (1953), European Convention on, 9–10

Inforce Foundation, 53

intercommunal relations/discussions: displaced persons/ refugees, 38; European Court of Human Rights, 76–78; overcoming constitutional provisions, 2–3; politics of, 19, 22; Third Vienna Agreement, 61; Turkey invasion and occupation, 27, 29; Turkish attempts to redefine, 51–52; Turkish Cypriot withdrawal from government, 1, 32

International Committee of the Red Cross (ICRC), 32–33, 50–51

International Convention on Civil and Political Rights, 80

International Court of Justice, 11, 24, 83

International Criminal Court, 9, 35, 80

international law: human rights and, 8–9; on missing persons, 53–56; political expediency and, 24; puppet states in, 31–32; Turkish colonization policy, 83–84; Turkish noncompliance, 56–59; UN violations of, 34–35

International Real Estate Federation, 75

intolerance, 13–14

Isaak v. Turkey, 45–46

Islam, 5, 83, 87

Israel, 73–74, 83

Jansen, Michael, 85, 87

Japanese war crimes trial (1946), 8

Jewish minorities, 35

Karpasia (village), 61

Karpass Peninsula, 3, 34, 60, 73, 83, 120 n. 5:12

Kasapis, Andrew, 119 n. 5:4

killings and murder. *See* torture, inhuman treatment, murder

Kormakitis (village), 60–61, 120 n. 5:12

Kurdish PKK, 120 n. 6:2
Kykkos Monastery, 89
Kyrenia (district), 4, 21, 60, 61, 77, 87, 120 n. 5:12
Kyrenia castle, 86

Laakso, Rapporteur J., 81, 84
Lapithos (village), 87
"law 35", 85
Lebanon, 61
Lippe-Weidenfeld, Alfred zur, 88
Loizidou, Titina, 21, 77
Loizidou v. Turkey, 20–21, 35, 57, 73, 75, 77, 79–80
London Agreement (1959), 1, 17, 91–92
looting and destruction, 4, 41–42, 70, 75
Lusignan family/dynasty, 5
Lythrangomi (village), 88

"Magna Carta" of human rights, 7–8
Makarios III, Archbishop of Cyprus, 117 n. 4:1
Malik, Charles, 8
Marathovouno (detention camp), 46
Maronite Cypriots: constitutional status, 118 n. 4:5; as "enclaved" Cypriots, 60–62; enclaved locations, 120 n. 5:12; fate following invasion, 3; protecting cultural heritage of, 86–87
Marty, Dick, 67
medical care, 4, 45, 60–64
missing persons: accounting for, 46, 119 n. 5:1, 119 n. 5:4; addressing the issue of, 49–51; addressing Turkish violations, 20; identification of remains, 3; international law and, 53–56; Turkish non-compliance, 56–59; UN Committee on Missing Persons, 51–53. *See also* displaced persons/refugees
monasteries: Apostolos Andreas, 60, 65; Kykkos Monastery, 89;

looting and destruction of, 86–87; Monastery of St. Andrew, 121 n. 6:21; Monastery of St. Barnabas, 121 n. 6:21; Sourp Magar, 87. *See also* religion/ religious minorities
Morphou (city), 4
Muller, A., 57
Muslim presence in Cyprus, 5, 83
Mycenaean Greeks, 5

National Security Agency (NSA), 1
national sovereignty. *See* sovereignty
NATO. *See* North Atlantic Treaty Organization (NATO)
Naturalization Act of 1975 (TRNC), 81–82
Nicola, Katerina and Vassilis, 39
Nicosia, 32, 46, 61, 78–79, 88
non-governmental organizations (NGOs): Asme-Humanitas report, 44, 46, 66–67; ethnic separation policy, 22; evidence of ethnic cleansing, 35–39; evidence of human rights violations, 92; human rights role, 9
North Atlantic Treaty Organization (NATO), 1
NSA. *See* National Security Agency (NSA)
Nuremberg War Crimes Trial (1945), 8, 35–36

Orams, David and Linda, 78–79
Organization for Security and Co-operation in Europe (OSCE), 6, 12–16
Ottoman Empire (1571-1878), 5, 35, 82, 86
Ozgur, Ozger, 83

Palestine, 83
Pineiro, Paolo Sergio, 80
Prevention of Discrimination and Protection of Minorities, 27
Prevention of Torture, Inhuman and Degrading Treatment or

Punishment (1989), Convention on, 10
prisoners of war (POW), 44, 50, 54, 59, 119 n. 4:22
Property Commission (TRNC), 71–74
Property Compensation Commission, 66, 78, 120 n. 6:3
property rights/law: court judgments, 75–79; European Court of Justice, 13; *Loizidou v. Turkey*, 20–21, 35, 57, 75, 77, 79–80; protection of property rights, 74–75; *Xenidis-Aresti v. Turkey*, 73, 75, 78. *See also* confiscation of property

racism, EU protections from, 13–14
rape and forced prostitution, 4, 43–44
refugees. *See* displaced persons/refugees
religion/religious minorities: desecration of churches, 86–87; destruction and looting of sites, 42, 86–87; ethnic cleansing based on, 35–36, 40, 42–44; EU protection of, 33–34; following invasion and occupation, 4, 8–9; human rights violations, 19–20, 28, 31, 47, 51, 81, 92; restricting practice of, 64–65. *See also* cultural heritage
Republic of Cyprus. *See* Cyprus, Republic of
resettlement programs, 4. *See also* ethnic cleansing; Turkish settlers
Riesen, M., 57
Rizokarpasso (village), 120 n. 5:12
Roman Empire (30 B.C.-330 A.D.), 5
Rome Treaty (1957), 12
Roosevelt, Eleanor, 7–9
rule of law: applied to human rights, 10; Cyprus as test for, 31–33, 92–93; Cyprus commitment to, 15; as OSCE foundation, 14
rules of war, 8–9
Russia, 7, 14

Saudi Arabia, 83
schools/education of children, 4, 61–62, 64–66
Sener, Abdullatif, 73
Serbia, 35
slave trade, human rights and, 8–9
society. *See* community; families
Solomou and Others v. Turkey, 45–46
Sourp Magar (monastery), 87
sovereignty: concept of, 8–9, 14; foreign intervention and, 32; of foreign military bases, 1; human rights and, 10, 32, 59; recognizing Cyprus, 1–2, 24–27, 33

Talat, Mehmet Ali, 83
Third Vienna Agreement (1975), 61, 64
Tokyo War Crimes Trial (1946), 8, 35
torture, inhuman treatment, murder: British violations in Cyprus, 16–17; of "enclaved" Cypriots, 62–65; as ethnic cleansing, 43–46; European Convention on, 10; following invasion, 4, 28, 36, 51; forensic evidence of, 53
tourism, 4, 42, 73
Treaty of Accession to the European Union (2003), 2, 15–16
Treaty of Amsterdam, 12–13
Treaty of Establishment (1960), 84
Treaty of Guarantee, 31–32
Treaty of the European Union, Founding, 12–13, 21
Trimithi (village), 87
tri-partite independence agreement, 1

TRNC. *See* "Turkish Republic of Northern Cyprus" (TRNC)

Turkey: Annan V Plan, 17–18; colonization policy, 82–84; Cypriot independence agreement, 1, 17; discrimination against minorities, 33–35; "domestic remedies law", 71–73, 120 n. 6:2; EU accession negotiations, 2, 5, 12–13, 21–22, 74, 93; getting "off the hook" in Cyprus, 23–29, 51; invasion/occupation of Cyprus, 1–5, 16, 31–33; occupation forces, 120 n. 6:4; U.S. military assistance to, 18–19, 117 n. 3:6, 117 n. 3:13; violations of human rights treaties, 11–12, 18–21, 91–93

Turkey, Demades v., 78

Turkey, Eleni Foka v., 34, 66

Turkey, Isaak v., 45–46

Turkey, Loizidou v., 20–21, 35, 57, 73, 75, 77, 79–80

Turkey, Solomou and Others v., 45–46

Turkey, Varnava and Others v., 55–56

Turkey, Xenidis-Aresti v., 73, 75, 78

Turkish Army, 3–4, 31–32, 39–40, 42–44, 51, 54, 61

Turkish Cypriots: ethnic cleansing of, 36; migration following invasion, 4, 81; tri-partite independence agreement, 1; withdrawal from Cyprus, 1–2, 32

Turkish Federated State of Cyprus, 70, 117 n. 4:2

"Turkish Republic of Northern Cyprus" (TRNC): confiscation of property, 70–73; creation as puppet state, 27–28, 117 n. 4:2; execution of captives, 50–51; illegality in international law, 31–32, 38; Naturalization Act of 1975, 81–82; recognizing legitimacy of, 51, 66, 72, 76, 78,

86, 89; Turkish settler impact on, 82–83

Turkish Revenge Brigade, 119 n. 5:6

Turkish settlers: addressing the issue of, 81–82; confiscation of property, 69–71; property sales to, 74; Turkey colonization policy, 82–84

United Cyprus Republic, 82

United Nations: Committee on Missing Persons, 51–53; Cyprus membership, 15–16; Cyprus resolutions, 26–29, 32–33; evidence of ethnic cleansing, 35–39; internationalization of Cyprus Problem, 25–29; involvement in Cyprus Problem, 18–19; Turkish colonization policy, 83–84; Turkish non-compliance, 56–59; Universal Declaration of Human Rights, 7–9

United Nations Educational, Scientific and Cultural Organization (UNESCO), 85, 88–90

United Nations Peacekeeping Force in Cyprus (UNFICYP), 1, 45, 56, 60–61, 64–65, 68, 88

United Nations secretary general: Annan V Plan, 1–2, 17–18, 22–23; failure to act, 37–39; human rights violations, 34–35

United Nations Security Council: Cyprus ceasefire and resolutions, 31–33; Cyprus resolutions, 26–29; on "enclaved" Cypriots issue, 68; response to ethnic cleansing, 35; Turkish invasion/occupation, 2

United Nations Universal Declaration of Human Rights (UDHR, 1948), 7–12, 69–70, 80

United States: citizens missing in Cyprus, 50, 119 n. 5:4; Declaration of Independence (1776), 7; failure to act in Cyprus, 37, 45;

foreign policy and security issues, 25–26, 115 n. 2:4; human rights violations, 34–35; involvement in Cyprus Problem, 18–19, 22, 91; military assistance to Turkey, 18–19, 117 n. 3:6, 117 n. 3:13; OSCE membership, 14; recovery of antiquities, 88–90

Van der Werff, Rapporteur, 85
Varnava and Others v. Turkey, 55–56
Venetian Republic (1191-1571), 5
Vitsada (detention camp), 46
Voni (detention camp), 46

Waldheim, Kurt, 88
war, human rights and rules of, 8–9
War and Cultural Heritage (Jansen), 87
weapons of mass destruction (WMD), 119 n. 4:22
Western Europe: institutional and procedural framework, 9–12; post-war human rights, 8–9
women. *See* families and society; rape and forced prostitution
World War I, human rights and, 8–9
World War II: post-war human rights, 7–9; war crimes trials, 8, 35–36

Xenidia-Aresti, Myra, 78
Xenidis-Aresti v. Turkey, 73, 75, 78
xenophobia, 13–14

Yasin, Mehmet, 85

Zurich Agreement (1959), 1, 91–92